JOURNEY TO
CROSSRAIL

RAILWAYS UNDER LONDON, FROM BRUNEL TO THE ELIZABETH LINE

STEPHEN HALLIDAY

The
History
Press

First published 2018

The History Press
The Mill, Brimscombe Port
Stroud, Gloucestershire, GL5 2QG
www.thehistorypress.co.uk

British Library Cataloguing in Publication Data.
A catalogue record for this book is available from the British Library.

ISBN 978 0 7509 8785 1

Typesetting and origination by The History Press
Printed in Turkey by Imak

CONTENTS

PREFACE

In the spring of 2014 I watched three programmes on BBC2 entitled *The Fifteen Billion Pound Railway*. They were about the construction of London's long-awaited main-line railway running across the capital from Reading and Heathrow airport in the west to Shenfield in Essex and Abbey Wood, near London's border with Kent. The programmes were amongst the best I had ever seen on television and I was particularly struck by the extraordinarily innovative engineering required to thread the tunnels through the maze of existing structures beneath London, and by the number of young women occupying key positions amongst the engineers involved in the project. I found this very encouraging. I live in Cambridge where I was also educated in the 1960s at a time when young women studying engineering at the university were rare indeed, less than 1 per cent of the total. The number is now approaching 25 per cent and rising.

I have previously written two books about London's Underground railways and it occurred to me, while watching *The Fifteen Billion Pound Railway*, that the programmes would be a useful starting point for anyone thinking of writing a book about Crossrail. In 2017 I was asked to write just such a book so my first debt is to the Cambridge University Department of Engineering whose library has discs of the programmes, which I was able to watch three years after the programmes were first transmitted.

One of the most pleasing anecdotes of the programmes concerned the tunneller whose career was about to end with Crossrail, having begun over fifty years earlier with the Victoria Line but who was handing on the family occupation to his two sons, also working on Crossrail. I have often come across dynasties of teachers, soldiers and doctors, but the last dynasty of tunnellers was surely Marc Brunel and his son Isambard Kingdom Brunel; what an act to follow!

The other sources upon which I have depended in writing this account of Crossrail include Cambridge University Library; the books and leaflets produced by Crossrail as the work has progressed, most notably *Platform for Design*, the generously illustrated account of the ways in which the new stations were designed; the London Transport Museum in Covent Garden; my friend from schooldays David Brice, who started to work for British Rail when it was called British Railways and before Dr Beeching set about wielding his axe and is still active in studying and advising on railway development in remote corners of the world; and Nick Firman, who is now head gardener at my Cambridge College. He patiently explained to me why sedum plants are suitable for station roofs (as at Whitechapel) and showed me one amongst the unrivalled flora that he has cultivated at Pembroke College, where he has worked for fifty-four years.

My aim has been to demonstrate that Crossrail is the latest chapter in a story of heroic railway engineering involving imaginative solutions to problems that require a blend of intelligence, imagination, determination and money which began with the great Victorians and continues to this day. I believe that the current generation of engineers, men and women, are worthy successors to Marc and Isambard Kingdom Brunel; George and Robert Stephenson; and the many thousands of workers, skilled and unskilled, most of them nameless, who realised their dreams.

Stephen Halliday,
Cambridge

INTRODUCTION

A LONG TIME COMING

For almost ten years Crossrail has been Europe's biggest and most ambitious construction project, and certainly the one with the longest and most controversial gestation. For the first time, main-line trains will be able to run from east to west beneath the streets of the capital without passengers having to change from one train to another. It will be possible, and soon commonplace, for someone to board a train in Essex or Kent and alight at Reading or at Heathrow airport. Why would any travellers, in such circumstances, wish to submit to the perils and uncertainties of the M25? Yet, as we will see, the idea of boarding a train in Reading (or Bristol) and travelling by Great Western Railway broad gauge beneath London to the heart of the city can be traced back a century and a half to the time (and the brain) of Isambard Kingdom Brunel (1803–59). So it is perhaps fitting that one of the tunnel-boring machines (TBMs) that has brought his idea to fruition bears the name of his wife while another bears that of his mother. And it is not only Brunel's legacy which the Crossrail project perpetuates. In preparing designs for the new stations for Crossrail the engineers, architects and artists have been following the precepts of Frank Pick (1878–1941) whose embracing of new ideas, from the London Transport Underground map to the adoption of new materials and models for stations, set new standards for public structures.

Isambard Kingdom Brunel against the launching chains of the SS *Great Eastern* at Millwall in 1857. (Photograph by Robert Howlett (1831–58))

The feats of engineering, finance and organisation which have brought about the project are themselves staggering. It will cost about £15 billion, with some of the money provided by the British government, some by Transport for London and some by the European Investment Bank; there will be contributions also from the owners of Heathrow airport and from the City of London. There will be 73 miles of railway line, 26 miles of which will be in new tunnels beneath London, with some beneath the Thames. The Crossrail Act, passed by Parliament in 2008, gave authority to Cross London Rail Links (CLRL) to build the system and to borrow the money to do it. The first shaft for the construction of the tunnels was sunk at Canary Wharf on 15 May 2009 in the presence of Transport Secretary Lord Adonis and the Mayor of London, Boris Johnson, and the tunnelling was finished at Farringdon on 23 May 2015 when the TBM *Victoria* broke into the eastern ticket hall of Farringdon's new station. The end of tunnelling was officially acknowledged on 4 June 2015 in the presence of Prime Minister David Cameron, with Boris Johnson once again in attendance as Mayor. On 23 February 2016 the Queen attended a ceremony at the newly completed Bond Street station and unveiled a plaque revealing that, from the time it enters service in autumn 2019, the line will be known as the Elizabeth Line, with a London Transport roundel and bar to match. It will increase the capacity of the rail system in central London by a much-needed 10 per cent.

THE NETWORK

The tunnels are doubled throughout their length, like the Channel Tunnel, so that trains travelling in opposite directions will not see each other when running underground. The main tunnel runs from Royal Oak, near Paddington, to Stepney before splitting into two branches. One emerges from the tunnel at Stratford and proceeds thence to Shenfield in Essex where it connects with the Great Eastern main line. The other goes to Canary Wharf on the Isle of Dogs and passes beneath the Thames and on to Abbey Wood, where south-east London meets Kent and Crossrail meets the North Kent Line. In the opposite, westerly direction the line runs to Hayes where one branch takes trains to Heathrow and the other goes to Reading to connect with the Great Western main line. At present about 1.4 billion passengers use the Underground system and it is anticipated that many of the 200 million who are expected to use Crossrail would otherwise have used the heavily congested Underground network in Central London, thus providing much needed relief for services like the Central, Northern and Piccadilly Lines. It is hoped that the inclusion of two destinations at each end of the system, Reading and Heathrow in the west, Shenfield and Abbey Wood to the east, will ensure a balanced flow of traffic in each direction.

The Crossrail network will comprise forty stations, of which seven will be central and will incorporate artworks commissioned from well-known artists, funded by the City of London Corporation and other sponsors. These are: Paddington, Bond Street, Tottenham Court Road, Farringdon, Liverpool Street, Whitechapel, Canary Wharf.

All the stations are incorporated in or accessible from the existing stations which bear their names though major reconstruction has been required in most cases. In the central area trains will run every two and a half minutes and, besides taking pressure off crowded lines in central London like the Central and Piccadilly Lines, journey times will be dramatically reduced as shown in the following examples:

	At present	With Crossrail
Abbey Wood to Heathrow	93 minutes	52 minutes
Paddington to Canary Wharf	34	17
Canary Wharf to Heathrow	55	39
Paddington to Tottenham Court Road	20	4

Some of the magnificent buildings at Canary Wharf, London's new financial district in the former docklands. (Fidocudeiro via Wikimedia Commons CC 3.0)

And these times do not reflect the fact that, for instance, passengers travelling from Reading, Shenfield or Abbey Wood will not need to change trains in the central area as Crossrail will be a through service.

There will be a new depot at Old Oak Common, close to the Great Western main line west from Paddington, and a smaller maintenance depot at Reading. A plan for an additional depot at the eastern end of the network at Romford was dropped after a motion was tabled by MPs in the House of Commons opposing the plan, largely on environmental grounds. An existing depot at Ilford will be used instead. The line will be operated by MTR Corporation (Crossrail) Ltd on behalf of Transport for London, which is also responsible, under the Mayor of London, for the London Underground, the London bus services, taxis, river transport, the Docklands Light Railway and the suburban rail routes into the capital known as London Overground. It also administers the congestion charge and the so-called Boris Bikes (actually the brainchild of Ken Livingstone, Boris Johnson's predecessor as Mayor), which are now sponsored by Santander. Services will begin from the central area in December 2018 and the entire system, from Reading and Heathrow to Shenfield and the rebuilt Abbey Wood station, is expected to be in operation by December 2019.

The so-called Boris bikes, which were actually conceived by Boris Johnson's predecessor as Mayor of London, Ken Livingstone, as a low-tech, pollution-free answer to London's congested streets. Now sponsored by Santander. (Chris Mckenna via Wikimedia Commons CC 4.0)

THE TUNNELLING AND UNDERGROUND CONSTRUCTION ACADEMY

A most welcome legacy of the Crossrail project is to be found in Ilford, east London, in the form of the Tunnelling and Underground Construction Academy which was completed in 2012 and trains employees in the skills and knowledge needed for the complex engineering work required to build, maintain and operate such a system. It is the only such institution in Europe and thereby helps to combat the shortages of engineering skills that are endlessly bemoaned by those who promote ambitious projects for which skilled staff are in short supply. More than 600 apprenticeships have been created to date, with an encouraging number of the places being taken up by young women. Fifteen thousand people have received training in such skills as the spraying of concrete lining for the construction of tunnels and stations. A laboratory has been created in the academy to study different types of tunnelling material. It will become the training centre for Elizabeth Line maintenance teams and for station staff, with twenty maintenance apprentices and a further 130 railway engineering apprentices. The facility will be managed on behalf of Transport for London by Prospects College of Advanced Technology which provides training on a nationwide basis for the engineering, aviation, rail and construction industries.

The Crossrail Act passed through Parliament in 2008 and eleven years later trains will begin to run. Compare that with the time it takes to decide to build an extra runway at Heathrow (or not, as the case may be); it's quite quick. But if we look more closely, it has taken more than a century and a half from Isambard Kingdom Brunel to Crossrail and the Elizabeth Line.

1

STEAM BENEATH
THE STREETS

'If you are going a very short journey you need not take your dinner with you, or your corn for your horse.'

Isambard Kingdom Brunel in evidence to a House of Lords Committee, 30 May, 1854

WHAT DO WE DO WITH THE SMOKE?

The gnomic assertion above by the celebrated engineer of the Great Western Railway formed part of Brunel's support for the idea of a main-line railway beneath the streets of London, which would enable his Great Western trains to transport passengers from Reading on the Great Western main line to the heart of the City of London without their having to endure the appalling congestion on London's inadequate roads. His ambition, moreover, was briefly realised before being overtaken by events and has lain dormant for over a century and a half, to be finally realised when the Elizabeth Line, formerly known as Crossrail, enters service in autumn 2019 – a century and a half too late for the great Victorian engineer. As we will see, there have been many false starts for the running of main-line rail services beneath London.

At the time that Brunel spoke, the only effective mechanism for moving passenger trains was the steam engine which, besides producing steam to drive the wheels, also emitted smoke which, in the confined space of an underground railway, could be intolerable. Electric engines were still a gleam in the eye of Michael Faraday (1791–1867) and more than three decades would pass before the City & South London Railway, in 1890, became the first underground railway to use this form of propulsion. It is now part of the Northern Line. Other methods had been tried, notably by Brunel himself.

MICHAEL FARADAY, ESQ. F.R.S. M.R.I. F.G.S. &c.

Michael Faraday, whose work on magnetism and electricity would eventually lead to an electric motor for railway trains, though not in time for the Metropolitan Railway. (H.W. Pickersgill via the National Library of Medicine)

A VACUUM-POWERED RAILWAY

In 1838 two engineers called Samuel Clegg and Jacob Samuda had patented the idea of a railway powered by atmospheric pressure. A cast-iron tube with a diameter of over a foot was laid between the rails. Within the tube was a piston attached by a rod to the underside of a train. At the end of the line a stationary steam engine pumped out the air in front of the piston, the resulting vacuum causing the piston, with the train attached to it, to be drawn along the rails. A demonstration railway 2 miles in length was built at Dun Laoghaire in Ireland, which made such an impression on Brunel that he asserted that 'Mere mechanical difficulties can be overcome', and he briefly adopted the system for the South Devon railway in the 1840s. The atmospheric pressure pumping house, now the home of a yacht club, may be seen in the small Devon community of Starcross, through which the railway ran between Exeter and Newton Abbot from 1846–47 at speeds of up to 70mph, much faster than a steam locomotive of the time could sustain. A section of the tube may be seen in the Great Western Railway Museum in Newton Abbot. Leather, beeswax and tallow were employed to create an airtight seal around the piston, but the beeswax and tallow melted in hot weather while the leather cracked

Vacuum power: the tube along which a locomotive, attached to a piston, would be drawn along Brunel's railway, if it weren't for the rats! (Wikimedia Commons CC SA 3.0)

Starcross pumping house, Devon, which provided the power for Brunel's
vacuum-powered railway. it is now the home of a yacht club. (Geof Sheppard via
Wikimedia Commons CC 3.0)

in cold weather and had to be softened by the application of oil. Rats
found the oily leather appetising and ate it, destroying the vacuum.
In a further experiment on a railway between Croydon and Epsom
the tube provided a popular home for more rats, who enjoyed eating
the leather as much as their cousins in Devon had done. The South
Devon Railway was 20 miles in length, more than twice as long as the
underground line that Brunel had in mind from Paddington to the
City, so if it had been made to work then Brunel's proposal for a main-
line railway beneath London would have been realised. But the rats
caused the experiment to be abandoned in 1847 after only a year and
with it went the chance of providing a steam- and smoke-free means
of propelling trains beneath the streets of London.

JOSEPH PAXTON'S GREAT VICTORIAN WAY

Despite these setbacks the 'atmospheric' form of propulsion rallied when it was proposed for two ambitious schemes to solve Victorian London's transport problems. One, the Crystal Way, was that of an architect called William Moseley, who planned to build a railway 12ft beneath the streets, linking St Paul's Cathedral in the City with Oxford Circus and Piccadilly Circus in the West End. Above the tracks would be a wrought-iron highway from which the trains beneath would be visible to pedestrians, who would also be able to visit rows of shops enclosed within a glass arcade – in effect a shopping arcade protected from the foul atmosphere of the capital with its smoke, fog and defective sewers. A similar arcade, also vacuum powered, though above ground, was proposed by Sir Joseph Paxton (1801–65) whose groundbreaking use of standard prefabricated components in cast iron and glass in the Crystal Palace for the Great Exhibition of 1851 had at first been condemned and

Joseph Paxton's use of prefabricated components for the Crystal Palace made possible the Great Exhibition of 1851 and inspired later designers, including those of Crossrail. His design for a great Victorian way encased in glass was less successful. (*The Illustrated London News*)

later applauded. The techniques, sophisticated at the time, were later used for the conservatory on Canary Wharf Crossrail station, as described in chapter 8. The Parliamentary Select Committee on Metropolitan Communications was impressed by the ingenuity of the schemes but deterred by the huge cost of £34 million – think billions in twenty-first-century values.

The Crystal Palace at its new home in Sydenham, where it was relocated after being dismantled and moved from the Great Exhibition site in Hyde Park. It was destroyed in a spectacular fire on 30 November 1936. (Philip Henry Delamotte, via Wikimedia Commons)

'WHAT WE PROPOSE TO DO
IS TO HAVE NO FIRE'

Brunel's solution, as expressed in his evidence to the House of Lords, was an engine that would build up sufficient heat and steam before entering the underground section of the line so that it could complete its subterranean journey without the need to burn more smoke-creating coal. Hence his expression to the House of Lords Committee which opened this chapter: 'If you are going a very short journey you need not take your dinner with you, or your corn for your horse.' The engineer to the line, John Fowler, was equally emphatic in his evidence to the Parliamentary Committee which was considering the matter, informing them that locomotives could continue to run for some time after the fire had been extinguished:

> What we propose to do is to have no fire ... to start with our boiler charged with steam and water of such capacity and such pressure as will take its journey from end to end and then, by arrangement at each end, to raise it up to its original pressure ... neither myself nor Mr Brunel nor any engineer would consider this as a matter of doubt. It is a mere practical mode of working.

John Fowler (1817–98) was one of the most prominent engineers of the Victorian age and possibly the most highly paid. Born near Sheffield, he trained on the Aire & Calder Navigation and on many railway schemes before being appointed Chief Engineer to the proposed Metropolitan Railway in 1853. He was later engineer also to the District Railway (now the District Line, with the Metropolitan and the District eventually being joined to form the Circle Line) and the Hammersmith & City Line. He was also consulted on railway projects in Algeria, Australia, Belgium, France and the USA. He became the youngest president of the Institution of Civil Engineers in 1865 and was also Chief Engineer to the Forth Railway Bridge. Fowler's earnings were legendary. He incurred the wrath of the equally colourful Sir Edward Watkin (1819–1901) in connection with Fowler's work on the Metropolitan of which Watkin was chairman, earning the rebuke:

John Fowler: highly paid engineer to the Metropolitan, District and many other railways who incurred the wrath of Sir Edward Watkin for his enormous fees. (Lock & Whitfield, Wikimedia Commons CC 4.0)

Robert Stephenson (1803–59) was one of the greatest locomotive engineers of the age, the designer of *Rocket* and builder of 'Fowler's Ghost', whose failure he did not live to see. (Tagishsimon, via Wikimedia Commons CC 3.0)

No engineer in the world was ever so highly paid ... you have set an example of charge [*sic*] which seems to have largely aided in the demoralisation of professional men of all sorts who have lived upon the suffering shareholders for the past ten years.

Fowler had been paid over £150,000 by the Metropolitan and a further £330,000 by the District Railway, huge sums at any time and monstrous in the nineteenth century, so Watkin had a point.

Such a locomotive was duly designed by Fowler and built in the workshops of the even more eminent engineer Robert Stephenson (1803-59), who had earlier designed the famous *Rocket*. The locomotive, which became known as 'Fowler's Ghost', stored energy by heating up bricks. The energy was gradually released into the water, creating enough steam power to propel the train for 7 miles. The locomotive which, at £4,518, was twice the cost of a normal engine, was delivered in 1861, two years after its builder's death, and tried out on the Great Western. But at the end of its 7-mile run it was dangerously overheated, emitting steam from every orifice and threatening to explode. It disappeared from history. Only one photograph of it survives.

OTHER SOLUTIONS TO LONDON'S TRAFFIC PROBLEMS: BOATS AND BUSES

In 1815 a steamboat service had been inaugurated between Greenwich and the City, with departures every fifteen minutes, but by the 1850s the Thames had become so polluted by London's sewage that it was a most unattractive thoroughfare. In 1855 the great scientist Michael Faraday described a journey along the Thames in a letter to *The Times* and commented, 'The appearance and smell of the water forced themselves at once upon my attention,' adding, 'surely the river which flows so many miles through London ought not to be allowed to become a fermenting sewer?' *Punch* followed up the letter with a cartoon of 'Michael Faraday presenting his card to Father Thames'. Fifteen years would pass before

Sir Joseph Bazalgette created the network of sewers which continues to serve London. (Courtesy of the late Derek Bazalgette CB)

the great network of sewers constructed by Sir Joseph Bazalgette (1819–91) cleaned up the river, and in the meantime the Thames did little to improve the lot of those who needed to move around the capital.

Sir Joseph Bazalgette (1819–91), like Marc Brunel, the father of Isambard, was long neglected in the pantheon of Victorian engineers. Like Brunel he was of French descent, though born in England, and between 1856 and 1889, in his capacity as Chief Engineer to the Metropolitan Board of Works, he designed and oversaw the construction of the system of intercepting sewers that turned the Thames from an open sewer to a clean river once the sewage of 3 million people had been taken off by his sewers to treatment works. The system is still in use today. About 10,000 people were employed on the system – the same number as employed on Crossrail. Bazalgette also built many of London's finest streets including Charing Cross Road, Northumberland Avenue, Garrick Street and Shaftesbury Avenue, as well as bridges across the Thames at Putney, Battersea and Hammersmith. He built the Victoria, Albert and Chelsea Embankments, the Victoria Embankment being designed to accommodate the underground Metropolitan & District Railway (now the District and Circle Lines). A full account of his life and work may be found in *The Great Stink of London: Sir Joseph Bazalgette and the Cleansing of the Victorian Metropolis* (The History Press).

A further attempt to overcome the problem of London's traffic was made by an enterprising coachbuilder called George Shillibeer (1797–1866). He took advantage of the construction of the New

Michael Faraday presenting his card to Father Thames. This is a view by John
Leech from *Punch* magazine of Faraday's encounter with the filthy condition of the
Thames following his journey along the stinking river.

George Shillibeer's omnibus was London's first bus service – a commercial failure that bankrupted its inventor but restored his fortunes when reinvented as a hearse.

Road between Paddington and the Angel to begin London's first bus service from Paddington Green to the Bank of England on 4 July 1829, but the project was doomed by the fact that the heavy traffic meant that it would have been quicker for the passengers to walk. Shillibeer went bankrupt and fled to France to escape his creditors, but was eventually arrested and, after a spell in a debtors' gaol, redesigned the bus as a hearse and recovered his fortunes. The New Road was soon renamed the Marylebone Road–Euston Road–Pentonville Road thoroughfare.

TRY THE CANAL

The Regent's Canal Company was established in 1812 by Act of Parliament and opened in 1820. It linked the Paddington arm of the Grand Junction (later Grand Union) Canal Company via Little Venice and Regent's Park to the River Thames at Limehouse Basin (as it still does) and was designed to convey freight on barges from the Midlands

and the north to east London and the London docks. By the 1840s the
company recognised that railways were threatening to take over the
freight traffic so in 1845 a group of businessmen proposed a scheme
to convert the canal into a railway, laying the rails along the canal bed
and through the web of tunnels beneath Maida Hill, Lisson Grove and
Islington. The company's prospectus explained that 'By the proposed
railway, passengers and goods will be brought into the heart of the
City at a great saving of time and expense' – the aim also of George
Shillibeer, Isambard Kingdom Brunel and, of course, Crossrail. The
railway company failed to raise the finance required and over the
next fifty years other schemes to lay a railway along or beside the
canal failed, in part because of objections to running a railway through
Regent's Park (they got a zoo instead). The Regent's Canal Company
continued to deliver freight to a dock in Regent's Park itself until the
Second World War, but by barge not by rail.

Little Venice: a tranquil feature of Regent's Canal, now the Grand Union Canal,
which survived attempts to turn the canal into a partly subterranean railway. (Author)

Limehouse Basin is where the canal meets the Thames. This is now a fashionable residential district though the lock-keeper's cottage may still be seen to the left of the picture. (Author)

THE THAMES TUNNEL

Other attempts to improve London's transport had focussed on River Thames crossings. Four toll bridges were built across the river at Vauxhall, Waterloo, Southwark and Hammersmith and in 1843 one of the most extraordinary engineering achievements of the century was completed. This was the Thames Tunnel between Wapping and Rotherhithe, which was built using a tunnelling shield invented by Sir Marc Brunel (1769–1849), the less well-known but equally gifted father of Isambard Kingdom Brunel (1806–59) who supervised the work as resident engineer. There is no doubt that the son inherited the father's imagination and his engineering expertise. Born in France, Marc fled the French Revolution and in 1793 became the official engineer to the city of New York. In 1799 he came to England and invented a process for the mechanisation of the production of ships' blocks, which guided the ropes of the Royal Navy's sailing ships.

It was adopted by the Admiralty and, after much prevarication by the admirals, Marc was paid £5,000 for the process, which enabled him to be released from a debtors' gaol. He invented a typewriter, a knitting machine and a boot-making machine and built the floating docks at Liverpool. But his greatest and most enduring achievement was the Thames Tunnel, built by his tunnelling shield, which he was inspired to build by observing the operations of the *Teredo navalis*, a mollusc known as a shipworm, which tunnelled into the wood of warships, its excrement hardening into a solid lining behind it and preventing the collapse of the tunnel.

The shield was a rectangular frame divided into three levels, or floors. On each level were cells, each large enough to accommodate a man with a pick and shovel. The men, known as 'miners', hacked away at the surface before them, protected by the frame from falling debris. When each of the men had cleared about 6in the shield was forced forwards by screw jacks and the mining began again. A conveyor belt removed the debris and bricklayers, following the miners, lined the space they had excavated.

Marc Brunel (1769–1849), the famous father of a more famous son. His invention of the tunnelling shield paved to way for all subsequent tunnelling ventures, including Crossrail. (Engraving by by G. Metzeroth, c. 1880)

Holes bored in wood by *Teredo navalis* or shipworm. A menace to wooden ships, the activities of this strange mollusc inspired Marc Brunel's invention of the tunnelling shield. (rosser1954 via Wikimedia Commons CC 3.0)

400M IN EIGHTEEN YEARS

The tunnel, almost 400m long, took eighteen years to complete. Progress was interrupted by mishaps including equipment failures, bankruptcy, inundations (one of which nearly drowned Isambard Brunel) and accidents to the miners whose hazardous work in insanitary conditions made them vulnerable to illness as well as injury. More than 100 of them died. At one particularly delicate point during the operation, following the collapse of the tunnel, Isambard, fresh from escaping drowning, was lowered into the river seated in a diving bell (accompanied by his redoubtable mother, Sophia!) to examine the damage. The water was kept beneath them by the pressure of the air in the bell. He located the breach in the tunnel roof and arranged for it to be sealed with sacks of clay. This operation was repeated several times. Some of the water was then pumped from the tunnel, which he entered on a punt, proceeding to a point close to where the shield was to be found. He then crawled across a bank of slime to the shield itself and, by candlelight, ascertained that it could be repaired and repositioned. He then returned and arranged for operations to recommence. That's a 'hands-on' Victorian engineer!

In 1841 Marc was knighted by Queen Victoria at the suggestion of her husband, Prince Albert, who was impressed by the enterprise shown by the engineer and thought it would encourage him in the final stages of the long and challenging project. The tunnel entered service as a foot tunnel on 25 March 1843, amidst much rejoicing. The cheering crowds observed a policeman wearing a medal that signified he had fought at Waterloo leading the long procession through the tunnel to the strains of Handel's 'See the Conquering Hero Comes', and the occasion inspired the following verse from one John Morgan:

A diving bell of the kind used by Isambard Brunel, accompanied by his mother, to descend into the Thames, inspect the source of the tunnel breach and direct the insertion of bags of clay to seal it. (Freshwater and Marine Image Bank)

The great big Duke of Wellington in splendour on does reel,
And through the tunnel he will go, to buy some pickled eels,
Both horse and man can go by land, oh what a pretty game,
From Rotherhithe to Wapping, underneath the River Thames.

This poem, absent from all known anthologies of English verse, is the only known record of the Iron Duke's supposed devotion to the Cockney delicacy of pickled eels!

Prince Albert, Queen Victoria's much-loved consort, was impressed by the enterprise and resolution shown by Marc Brunel in building the Thames tunnel and advised the Queen to grant him a knighthood. (William Edward Kilburn (1818–91))

Marc Brunel's tunnelling shield, the ancestor of all tunnelling shields since designed.

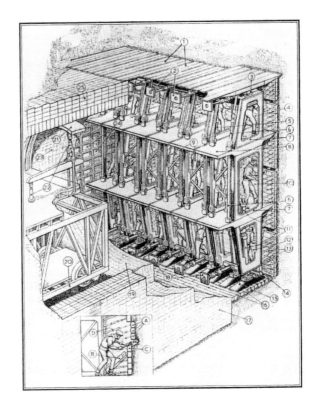

A contemporary engraving showing the tunnelling shield in use beneath the Thames.

The procession that marked the opening of Brunel's Thames tunnel. This contemporary illustration, from a German magazine, indicates the degree of foreign interest in the project , not just in Great Britain. (Johann Jacob Weber (Hrsg.), (1803–80))

A ROYAL VISIT

Four months later, in July 1843, an even grander scene saw Queen Victoria visit the Thames Tunnel. On that occasion, recorded by *The Illustrated London News*, a gallant stallholder selling silken goods in the tunnel emulated Sir Walter Raleigh and 'displayed his loyalty in a peculiar manner. All the silk handkerchiefs disposed on his stall for sale were removed and placed on the ground for Her Majesty to pass over.' They were then presumably sold to loyal subjects at an enhanced price.

Such was the novelty of the tunnel that 1 million people visited it in the three months which followed its opening – more than half the population of London at the time. Nevertheless, the tunnel was never profitable as a foot tunnel, and in 1865 it was bought by the East London Railway to carry its trains beneath the river, as it still does. It is one of the more neglected corners of the London Underground network, but it runs through the world's oldest tunnel beneath a river. Moreover Brunel's tunnelling shield, which made its construction possible, is the ancestor of the shields which later built London's

Son and resident engineer Isambard Brunel greets father and designer, Sir Marc Brunel, at the opening of the Thames tunnel. (Johann Jacob Weber (Hrsg.), (1803–80))

deep-level tubes, beginning with the City & South London Railway in 1890 (now the Northern Line), and of course, the Channel Tunnel and Crossrail.

WHERE DO THE PASSENGERS WANT TO GO?

The construction of the Thames Tunnel, despite its difficulties, was eventually to prove a seminal event in the development of underground railways throughout the world but in the meantime the main-line railway companies had to find a way of delivering their passengers from their main-line termini on the periphery of the metropolis to the business, financial and political centres of the City and Westminster. In 1836 Robert Stephenson, who was building the London to Birmingham Railway, proposed to construct its terminus

Covent Garden market happily escaped being undermined by Robert
Stephenson's projected underground steam railway running from Euston to the
Thames. (Nathan Meijer via Wikimedia Commons CC 2.0)

Savoy pier: a tranquil scene undisturbed by Robert Stephenson's plans for a railway
terminus served by steam trains. (The Lud via Wikimedia Commons)

at Savoy Wharf on the north bank of the Thames, a site now occupied by the Savoy Hotel. He proposed to build a tunnel beneath Gower Street and Covent Garden to avoid disruption to roads and properties on the surface. The railway eventually settled for a terminus at Euston. Stephenson was aware of the disastrous collapses which had befallen the incomplete Thames Tunnel on which the Brunels were still labouring and was deterred by the prospect of compensation claims from wealthy property owners in Covent Garden and Bloomsbury if similar problems had occurred with his railway tunnel. Had it gone ahead, this proposal to run main-line trains beneath London's streets would have predated Crossrail by over 180 years and would possibly, disastrously, have made use of the engine Stephenson designed for Brunel and referred to above as 'Fowler's Ghost'.

In 1846 a body of commissioners was appointed by Parliament to consider a number of railway projects which had come before them. Upon hearing Stephenson's evidence about his earlier proposal the commissioners concluded that, in order to avoid the disruption that would inevitably accompany such a plan 'on the North of the Thames, no railway now before Parliament or projected' would be permitted to penetrate beyond the New Road (now the Marylebone Road–Euston Road–Pentonville Road thoroughfare). As a result, a chain of main-line termini was constructed north and west of this road from Paddington in the west to Marylebone, Euston, St Pancras and King's Cross in the east. By 1850 these termini were receiving hundreds of thousands of passengers who wished to be in Westminster or the City, both some miles distant by increasingly congested roads.

2

THE WORLD'S FIRST UNDERGROUND RAILWAY

'Utopian and one which, even if it could be accomplished, would certainly never pay.'

The Times's view of the prospects of the Metropolitan Railway, now the Metropolitan Line.

CHARLES PEARSON'S ARCADE RAILWAY

A more promising solution was proposed by Charles Pearson (1794–1862), solicitor to the City of London. Pearson's scheme took advantage of the fact that the livestock market at Smithfield and its accompanying 'noxious trades' (slaughterhouses and tanning works) were being removed to an area to the north of King's Cross called Copenhagen Fields, leaving the site of the former cattle and sheep pens to be redeveloped, as well as the route the animals had taken to market along Farringdon Road. The livestock market had prospered since the Middle Ages, but by the 1840s over 100,000 cattle and 1.5 million sheep annually were, in the words of *Farmers' Magazine*,

Old Smithfield market in 1824, still trading as a livestock market before its removal in 1855 to Copenhagen Fields to the north of the old site. (Jacques-Laurent Agasse (1767–1849))

being 'violently forced into an area of five acres, in the very heart of London, through its narrowest and most crowded thoroughfares'. The Lord Mayor complained of the multitude of 'loose, idle and disorderly persons' that the market attracted and the frightened animals were sometimes goaded by their drivers into panic in the hope that they would run amok and destroy property on their route, coining the phrase 'bull in a china shop'. The livestock market was replaced by a market for slaughtered meat, which it remains.

Pearson observed, with commendable foresight, that building more roads like the New Road would simply generate more traffic, and was instead an advocate of cheap trains to allow working families to move to more salubrious homes beyond the centre of the metropolis. In place of roads he proposed the construction of an 'arcade railway' which would take advantage of the width of the redeveloped Farringdon Road. It would lie beneath street level but be open to

New Smithfield market, 1872, by which time it was, as it remains, for slaughtered meat only in a building designed by the city architect Sir Horace Jones. It was opened in 1868. (Oxyman via Wikimedia Commons CC 2.0)

the air in the middle of Farringdon Road, with lanes for pedestrians and surface vehicles, like horses and carts, on either side of the railway. Being open to the atmosphere it would be possible to use steam engines. A new railway terminus would be built at Farringdon, close to the new Smithfield Market, and the terminus would be convenient for the offices and banks of the City nearby. The station would also have a separate facility for handling freight travelling to and from the meat market overnight. Pearson described his proposal as:

A great trunk line capable of maintaining a frequent, rapid, punctual and cheap intercommunication between the City and the suburbs without courting dangerous collisions by commingling on the same lines creeping goods wagons with flying expresses and mixing up erratic excursionists with the migratory population of the City.

When Pearson (pictured right) first proposed his scheme in 1852, it was embraced with enthusiasm by the Great Northern Railway, since it would enable it to convey its passengers beyond its new London terminus and headquarters at King's Cross to the heart of the City, where they wanted to go. This would have run main-line trains beneath the streets of the city 150 years before Crossrail. The Great Northern set aside £170,000 to contribute to the share capital of Pearson's Arcade Railway, but unfortunately the money was embezzled by one of its employees, called Leopold Redpath, who used it for 'the furnishings of magnificent houses and the purchase of articles of vertu'. Redpath was one of the last convicts to be transported to Australia for his crimes in 1858, where he thrived.

Pearson's Arcade Railway was never built as he intended it but his idea was drawn to the attention of the Parliamentary Committee, which had also been considering the alternative proposal which Brunel had advocated. Brunel's scheme's purpose is described in the cumbersome title of the Bill presented to Parliament in 1854: 'The Metropolitan Railway, Paddington and the Great Western Railway, the General Post Office, the London and North Western Railway and the Great Northern Railway'.

The proposed line would run beneath the New Road, linking the main-line stations at Paddington, Euston and King's Cross – the General Post Office at St Martin's le Grand being included in the plan to secure the support of the Postmaster General, Rowland Hill, who had introduced the Penny Post ten years earlier. By linking the main-line stations (later joined by St Pancras and Marylebone) together, the

King's Cross station was completed in 1852 as the terminus of the Great Northern Railway, but the passengers needed to go on into the city. The clock was originally used in the Great Exhibition of 1851, housed in Paxton's Crystal Palace. (Mattbuck via Wikimedia Commons CC SA 3.0)

Convicts awaiting transportation to Australia, with Leopold Redpath perhaps amongst them. (*The Illustrated London News*)

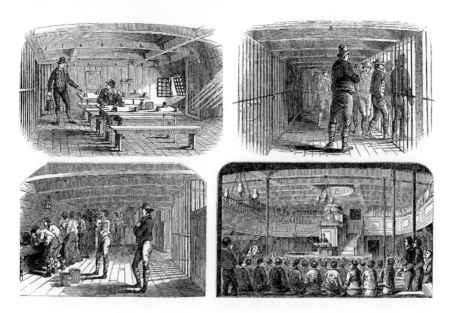

underground railway (henceforward called the Metropolitan Railway) would facilitate travel between those stations but it would not have taken them to the City itself. By joining the Metropolitan Railway to Pearson's railway along the Farringdon Road, the passengers from all the main-line stations could be taken directly to their destinations in the City. In the words of the Parliamentary Committee, 'The different metropolitan railway termini should be connected by railway with each other, with the docks, the river and the Post Office so as to take all through traffic off the streets.' Moreover, the work 'should be carried out by private enterprise'. The river and the docks would have to wait, but this was the blueprint for the world's first underground railway, the Metropolitan Railway from Paddington to Farringdon which was to lend its name to numerous other underground railways in the world, starting with the Paris Métro.

The Paris Métro was the first underground railway system to copy the name of London's Metropolitan Railway, but not the last. (Bellomonte via Wikimedia Commons)

Rowland Hill, inventor
of the penny post and all
modern postal systems, whose
support helped to create the
Metropolitan Railway and
was one of its first passengers.
(Author)

CONSTRUCTION BEGINS

Construction of the world's first underground railway began in 1861, following a line beneath Marylebone Road and Euston Road before turning south beneath the Farringdon Road. It began at Paddington and served two other main-line stations, at Euston, the station there being called Gower Street at the time, now Euston Square, and King's Cross (soon joined by St Pancras and later by Marylebone) with additional stops at Edgware Road, Baker Street and Great Portland Street as well as the City Terminus at Farringdon.

It was built by the 'cut and cover' method. A trench was built along the New Road and Farringdon Road, the line was installed and then covered by concrete so that the road came back into use. It was built to accommodate main-line trains, whereas the later deep tubes were built to a smaller gauge. To this day the carriages on the Metropolitan, District, Hammersmith & City and Circle Lines are substantially higher than those on the 'tubes' like the Northern, Central, Bakerloo and Piccadilly Lines.

Its construction was initially the object of scepticism, followed by curiosity and, eventually, admiration. In 1861, as work began, *The Times* described the project as:

> Utopian and one which, even if it could be accomplished, would certainly never pay. The whole idea has been generally associated with plans for flying machines, warfare by balloons, tunnels under the channel and other bold but hazardous propositions of the same kind … an insult to common sense.

Everything *The Times* disparaged was eventually to come to pass, but despite its scepticism it, and other publications, followed the progress of the line with great interest. When the River Fleet, which runs beside the line beneath Farringdon Road, burst in upon the construction

Construction work in progress for the Metropolitan Railway south of King's Cross. (P. Justyne)

Daniel Gooch, Brunel's locomotive engineer whose design for a locomotive which would consume its own steam and smoke was only moderately successful. (Leslie Ward)

works, *The Illustrated London News* sent an artist to record the devastation and pronounced the scene 'well worthy of a visit'. But when the line finally opened in January 1863 even *The Times* had changed its mind, pronouncing it 'the great engineering triumph of the day'. The new railway had three rails, as is evident from contemporary drawings. Two were designed to accommodate standard-gauge locomotives and rolling stock of 4ft 8½in – the gauge used by George Stephenson to build his first railway from Stockton to Darlington and still used by most of the world's railways. It is also known as Stephenson Gauge. The third rail was laid to accommodate the broad gauge (7ft) adopted by Brunel for the Great Western Railway and which remained in use until 1892. The third rail enabled the Great Western to run main-line trains from Reading and the west through to Farringdon as well as providing locomotives and rolling stock for the early months of the Metropolitan's own shuttle service.

THE WORLD'S FIRST UNDERGROUND RAILWAY

On 9 January 1863 the first trains carried the directors and 700 of their guests from Paddington to Farringdon. Amongst them was the Postmaster General, Rowland Hill. But the Prime Minister, Lord Palmerston, was absent. He had been invited, but the 79-year-old statesman replied that he 'wished to remain above ground a little longer'. He died two years later. The line opened to the public the following day, using Great Western broad-gauge rolling stock. 'Fowler's Ghost' having failed, the trains were hauled by locomotives designed by the locomotive engineer Daniel Gooch (1816–89), who worked with Brunel on the Great Western. The locomotives were fuelled by coke and designed to consume their own smoke and to condense the steam and return it to the tank. The condensing mechanism was quite successful, but the smoke remained obstinately unconsumed, with consequences we will examine later in the chapter. The locomotives were named after unpleasant insects (*Mosquito* and *Hornet*) and tyrants (*Kaiser* and *Czar*).

Lord Palmerston (1784–1865), the ageing Prime Minister, whose wish to 'remain above ground a little longer' prompted him to decline the invitation to join the first train passing along the underground railway. He died two years later.

Lord Palmerston.

The Metropolitan Railway at Praed Street, approaching Baker Street station, shortly after the line entered service. Note the third rail, designed to accommodate the GWR broad-gauge locomotive and carriages, which were soon to be withdrawn and replaced by Metropolitan rolling stock of standard gauge. (Samuel J. Hodson)

Charles Pearson had died in September 1862, four months before the opening of the railway he had promoted, but in accordance with his wishes the Metropolitan instituted workmen's trains at 5.30 and 5.40 a.m. with return fares of threepence. The line's popularity was immediate, with over 30,000 people using it from the first day. It was clear that the Metropolitan Railway needed to increase the frequency of its services. The passengers might have been a little less enthusiastic if they had known that the lights in the carriages were fuelled by gas, which was contained in tarpaulins on the carriage roofs and often surrounded by sparks from the locomotives. Health and safety were not paramount concerns of Victorian engineers or entrepreneurs!

THE GREAT WESTERN WITHDRAWS

The Great Western, which was running services direct from Reading to Farringdon as well as supplying the locomotives and carriages for the Metropolitan's shuttle service from Paddington to Farringdon, was reluctant to commit more of its locomotives and rolling stock to increase the frequency of the Metropolitan's service. It was also anxious when it learned that the Metropolitan was discussing with the Great Northern the possibility of running through trains from Hatfield and Hitchin to Farringdon. The directors of the Great Western announced that they would withdraw all services, leaving the line bereft of trains. The Metropolitan Railway directors managed to borrow some standard-gauge stock from the Great Northern as a temporary measure, making use of the standard-gauge tracks, and bought eighteen locomotives and thirty-four carriages of their own from the Manchester locomotive engineers Beyer & Peacock, who adapted a design they were building for Spanish and Portuguese railways. There was a temporary fall in passenger numbers following the Great Western's withdrawal but their bluff had been called and they eventually resumed the running of through trains, sharing the line with the Metropolitan's own services and the Great Northern's services from King's Cross. It would be another 145 years before Crossrail introduced such a service.

FURTHER INTO THE CITY

In the meantime the Metropolitan extended its services further into the heart of the City. By December 1865 it had reached Moorgate, with an intermediate station at Aldersgate (now Barbican). Aldersgate station was spanned by a particularly fine wrought-iron and glass roof which was damaged in the Second World War and removed in 1965, its loss being lamented in John Betjeman's 'Monody on the Death of Aldersgate Street Station':

> Snow falls in the buffet of Aldersgate station,
> Toiling and doomed from Moorgate Street puffs the train,
> For us of the steam and the gas-light, the lost generation,
> The new white cliffs of the City are built in vain.

The following year a further connection was made with the London, Chatham & Dover Railway's station at Ludgate Hill, close to the present site of the City Thameslink station on Holborn Viaduct. The original Smithfield Market goods station was connected to the line from Farringdon to City Thameslink but is now the site of a multi-storey car park for the market. The line was also used by the Great Northern to run freight trains across the river, forming a north–south link, and in 1868 the widened lines were laid beside the Metropolitan Railway tracks with a new tunnel beneath Clerkenwell to link Great Northern tracks at King's Cross with the London, Chatham and Dover lines. So by 1868, main-line freight and passenger trains could run north–south through London, partly underground. The passenger service ceased in the First World War but was reopened as Thameslink in 1988. Trains now run from Bedford to Brighton by this route.

THE LUDGATE-HILL STATION OF THE LONDON, CHATHAM, AND DOVER RAILWAY.

Ludgate Hill station, 1865. This was the London terminus of the London, Chatham & Dover Railway from 1865 until 1929 when it closed, though parts of the building survived until 1990. The nearby City Thameslink station, with services to Bedford and Brighton, lies close to the site of the former Ludgate Hill station. (*The Illustrated London News*)

City Thameslink station opened in 1988 close to the site of the former Ludgate Hill station to provide a main line link from stations to the north of London and southern destinations like Brighton. (sunil060902 via Wikimedia Commons CC SA 3.0)

THE LOCOMOTIVE PROBLEM

There remained the problem of the locomotives. The Stephenson design advocated by Brunel had failed, but John Fowler, the engineer to the line, secured an alternative from Daniel Gooch, Brunel's long-serving colleague on the Great Western. Gooch's design diverted the steam into an exhaust pipe which conveyed it, condensed, to a cold water tank for reuse. The design remained in use for a century but did nothing to dispel the smoke, which was a far more offensive hazard. Ventilator shafts were let into the tunnels from the roads above but these were very ineffective and the atmosphere in the tunnels was often poisonous. In 1879, a letter to *The Times* described it thus:

> The condition of the atmosphere was so poisonous that, though a mining engineer, I was almost suffocated and was obliged to be assisted from the train at an intermediate station. On reaching the open air I requested to be taken to a chemist close at hand. Without a moment's hesitation he said 'Oh, I see, Metropolitan Railway' and at once poured out a wine glass of what he designated Metropolitan Mixture. I was induced to ask him whether he often had such cases to which he rejoined 'Why bless you Sir, we often have twenty cases a day'.

As late as 1898 a Board of Trade Committee on Ventilation of Tunnels was told that about 550 passenger and goods trains were passing though the tunnels each day but the Metropolitan's General Manager, John Bell, assured the members that his company's employees were the healthiest railwaymen in the land and that the Great Portland Street station, one of the most noxious, was 'actually used as a sana-torium for men who had been afflicted with asthma and bronchial complaints'! In support of his employer Mr A. Langford, a driver, told the committee of his excellent health following thirty-four years of service but then spoilt his evidence by adding, superfluously, that only 'very seldom' was the smoke so thick as to render the signals invisible!

It was clear that, despite the confidence of John Bell and the more ambiguous testimony of driver Langford, there was a limit to the

Portland Road Underground station (now Great Portland Street station) with a train of celebrities approaching, in 1862, the year before the Metropolitan Railway opened. Its smoky atmosphere was particularly recommended for those with bronchial complaints, though only by the Metropolitan Railway's management! (*The Illustrated London News*)

extension of railways beneath the streets of the capital unless a source of power more benign than steam engines could be found.

MAIN-LINE TRAINS UNDER LONDON

So, in 2018 we will once again realise Isambard Kingdom Brunel's vision of running main-line trains beneath London, just as the Great Western did from Reading in 1863. Indeed the Metropolitan Railway itself never really thought of itself as an underground railway of the kind with which we have become familiar. A glance at its locomotives confirms that they were steam engines like any other except that they had an extra pipe which condensed the steam and took it back to the water tank rather than releasing it to the air. And they produced as much smoke as any other steam engine, with consequences for the health and comfort of the passengers that have already been noted. Moreover, the carriages are identical to many others of the time that ran into Euston, King's Cross and other main-line stations. The Metropolitan long thought of itself as a perfectly respectable surface train which, by painful necessity, had to run in a long tunnel. And that, more grandly, is more or less what Crossrail is.

A Metropolitan Railway carriage, indistinguishable from one used on main-line trains. Note the first- and third-class carriages, soon to disappear on the Victorian tubes but reintroduced on Crossrail. (Peter Skuce via Wikimedia Commons)

A Metropolitan Railway condensing locomotive heading for Baker Street station. Note the condensing pipe leading back to the tank. Unfortunately it didn't consume its own smoke as was hoped.

3

LONDON AT WAR

'The possibilities of a duplication of tubes on certain lines or some other means of providing an express service need exploring.'
County of London Plan, 1943.

TOO MANY PASSENGERS FOR COMFORT

In the years between the wars the Underground expanded into the northern suburbs of London in order to encourage long-distance commuters to use the services and buy season tickets. The Metropolitan Railway was the most successful in earning profits in this way, particularly from property development in places like Buckinghamshire.

But one effect of this policy, which also affected the Northern Line, was that trains became overcrowded, both north and south of the river, since by 1926 the Charing Cross branch of the Northern Line extended from Edgware and Highgate in the north to Morden in the south. The railway had printed posters encouraging Londoners to move from inner London to rural Edgware, where they could be 'Master of a small House and a large Garden, with moderate conveniences joined to them'. The residents of Hampstead, in particular, were unhappy about these developments, especially when they found that the trains were filled before they reached them.

In February 1931 a Mr W. Rushton wrote to *The Times* drawing attention to 'A grievance of Hampstead' and complaining that since the extension of the line to Highgate, 'The intelligentsia of Hampstead has the chagrin of witnessing the canaille of Highgate lolling at their ease while we have to hang on to our straps ... Is it fair?'

It was certainly fair as far as Sir Edgar Speyer was concerned. He had financed the completion of the Piccadilly Line and simply commented that 'straphangers meant dividends and those who had a complaint to make would find their angry feelings greatly smoothed if they became shareholders in the railway.'

By the mid 1930s *The Times* and other newspapers carried an almost continuous tide of correspondence about overcrowded trains, especially on the Hampstead branch of the Northern Line. On 4 November 1935 a correspondent from Hampstead complained that he had been one of eighty-eight passengers obliged to stand in one carriage and another added that during the evening peak travel period there were 'not less than sixty in every compartment. This is double the complement, the discomfort is extreme, the air vitiated, everyone fatigued.'

An element of humour is to be found in a complaint about overcrowding on a Central Line train when the correspondent explained how, when he failed to board one train, he allowed a human tide to carry him on to the next one:

On several occasions I have been one of a bunch of rejects and have had to wait for another train. At such times one's only chance of adding to the crush inside was to judge the speed of approach and jockey for position near a door. Once there I admit things are much easier; one only has to adopt a passive stance and a wave of surging humanity does the rest.

One correspondent, writing from the august precincts of The Athenaeum, suggested that the installation of parcel racks would help to ease the problem; he didn't say whether they would be for parcels or for prostrate passengers.

TAKING SHELTER FROM THE BLITZ

On 3 November 1940, as the Luftwaffe rained bombs on London at the height of the Blitz, the Home Secretary, Herbert Morrison, announced on the BBC that 'a new system of tunnels *linked to the London tubes* should be bored'. By the time he made the announcement, the Underground had become a huge air raid shelter with about 200,000 Londoners seeking refuge in them from the bombs. They were attended by an impressive array of services to make their lives tolerable, including: Tube Refreshment Specials – trains running round the system furnished with cocoa, cakes and other refreshments by J. Lyons and Co.; bunk beds on three tiers; lavatories; entertainments including CEMA (Council for the Encouragement of Music and the Arts), ENSA (Entertainment National Service Association), George Formby playing his ukulele on a platform above the tracks, ballroom dancing classes, and inter-shelter competitions for such occupations as darts; and a team of thirty-six doctors and 200 nurses dealing with everything from mosquito bites and grazed knees to childbirth.

Herbert Morrison (1888–1965) was born in Lambeth, the son of a police constable. He was blind in one eye almost from birth. He became active in Labour Party politics as a young man and was instrumental in making the party a dynamic force in London politics. He became Mayor of Hackney in 1920, and a member of the London County Council (LCC) in 1922, and the following year he entered Parliament as MP for Hackney South. He became Minister of Transport in the Labour government of 1929–31 and was responsible for creating the London Passenger Transport Board (a first step to public ownership of the Underground and London's buses) in that office. He lost his Parliamentary seat in 1931 and became Leader of the LCC, returning to Parliament in 1935. He lost to Clement Attlee in the party leadership election of that year. During almost the whole of the Second World War he served as Home Secretary and orchestrated the Labour victory in the General Election of 1945 when he made his second failed attempt to replace Attlee as leader of the party and hence Prime Minister. When Attlee resigned as leader of the

Herbert Morrison (1888–1965), Labour politician and wartime Home Secretary, ordered the construction of deep shelters whose mysterious entrances are still a feature of locations close to some Northern Line stations. (Photograph by Yousuf Karsh (1908–2002); Dutch National Archives via Wikimedia Commons))

party in 1955 Morrison came third in the election, Hugh Gaitskell being the successful candidate. In 1959 he became Lord Morrison of Lambeth and in 1965 he died, his ashes being scattered on the Thames outside County Hall, the headquarters of the LCC which Morrison had long dominated and which was replaced by the Greater London Council (GLC) shortly after Morrison's death.

Harmony did not always prevail in the shelters, despite Morrison's efforts to provide creature comforts. The following conversation was recorded in one shelter, initiated by an irascible old lady whose bed was close to the lavatory:

'Seventy-eight people want to go to the lavatory.'

'Can't you shut up you bleeding little hypocrite?'

'I want to go to sleep and these people keep on going to the lavatory.'

Nor did the Underground stations always offer complete protection from the bombs. Bounds Green station on the Piccadilly Line, and Balham on the southern part of the Northern Line, were both struck, with many victims. And in March 1943, in the worst incident of the Blitz, 173 people were killed, mostly trampled or suffocated, on the stairway leading down to Bethnal Green station on the Central Line.

MYSTERIOUS STRUCTURES

It was in these circumstances that Herbert Morrison made his announcement about the construction of 'Tunnels linked to the London Tubes'. Ten were planned and eight were built. Mysterious structures began to appear on the surface (where they remain) – but they were nothing to what was built beneath them. Of the total number built, seven were close to Northern Line stations and their buildings may still be seen on the surface at Belsize Park, Camden Down, Goodge Street, Stockwell, Clapham North, Clapham Common, and Clapham South; one was planned at the Oval station but abandoned because of difficult ground conditions. The other two planned were on the Central Line at Chancery Lane and St Paul's, though the latter was also abandoned for fear of damaging the foundations of St Paul's Cathedral.

The precise reason for their construction is not entirely clear. They were probably intended to afford additional, purpose-built accommodation for Londoners seeking refuge from the Blitz, though by the time they were completed in 1942 the Blitz had ended as Hitler turned his attention to Russia. They may also have been intended as a refuge for essential government services in the event of unknown 'terror weapons' raining down on the capital. Five of the shelters were opened to the public in 1944, when the bombing resumed in the form of the V-1 and V-2 weapons. But by the time the V-1 flying bombs and V-2 rockets reached London, France had been invaded by the Allies and the launch sites were gradually being overrun, so although they were terror weapons, they didn't seriously impede the business of government or affect the outcome of the war.

But the fact that the deep shelters were built close to the Northern Line and the Central Line suggests that there was also an intention, once the war was over, to link them together to provide additional capacity for those two lines which, as we have seen above, were the most overcrowded. Moreover, the size of the tunnel shelters suggests that they were intended, like Crossrail, to accommodate main-line rolling stock. The Northern and Central Lines, like the other tubes, have running tunnels which are just under 12ft (3.5m) in diameter. The tunnel shelters, by contrast are much larger than the ordinary running tunnels, with a diameter of 16½ft (5m), so although they would not have been large enough for a station without additional work, they could have accommodated main-line trains. Each shelter was designed to accommodate 8,000 people, giving a total capacity of 64,000 – about one third of those who sought shelter in Underground stations during the Blitz. By the 1940s electric trains were well established above as well as below ground. The prospect of running larger, faster trains alongside the crowded tube lines, stopping at fewer stations, was both feasible and attractive. Such a system exists in Paris in the form of the RER (*Resau Express Regional* or Regional Express Network) and in New York. But it was not to be for London. This was to be one of many false starts for main-line railways beneath London.

4

LONDON PLANS
FOR PEACE

'The war has given us a great opportunity.'
County of London Plan, 1943.

RECONSTRUCTING LONDON

In 1942 the government and the London County Council (LCC) began the preparation of a plan for the post-war reconstruction of London. The work was undertaken by John Forshaw, architect to the London County Council, and Patrick Abercrombie, Professor of Town Planning at University College, London. This showed commendable foresight since, while the outlook for victory looked more promising in 1942, it was still far from being assured. The County of London Plan, published in 1943 and known as the Abercrombie Report, is usually remembered for the new towns like Hemel Hempstead and Stevenage, which were to rehouse Londoners, and it was certainly ambitious. It began with the confident assertion that 'the war has given us a great opportunity' – the opportunity being provided by the Luftwaffe's destruction of much of London, including many slums. However, the destruction visited on the railways, especially the main-line railways, was substantial, and by 1945 the tracks, the freight facilities, locomotives and rolling stock were in very poor condition. During the war they had been the mainstay of the nation's transport, moving workers, troops, raw materials and weapons and had received little investment and much destruction.

The plan recognised this and drew attention to the poor connections between main line and Underground services. It deplored the pre-war tendency of the Underground to develop profitable commuter lines on the periphery of London rather than concentrating on improvement within the central area: 'Without thought for the total welfare of London they have pushed their lines out to the open country, encouraging uncontrolled speculative estate development.' The consequences, in the form of overcrowding, have been noted in chapter 3 and the trend had continued with the extension of the Central Line to Gants Hill and Epping in Essex though these lines

Sir Leslie Patrick Abercrombie gave his name to the County of London Plan. Its ambitious aims for post-war reconstruction were largely unrealised owing to financial constraints.

did not enter service until the war ended. It referred, in the quotation which opened the previous chapter, to the fact that, 'the possibilities of a duplication of tubes on certain lines or some other means of providing an express service need exploring', and we have seen that the construction of the deep shelters may have been an early step in that direction. The report also deplored the prevalence of railway viaducts, especially in South London, which they regarded as a source of dirt (from steam trains) and described as 'one of the chief causes of the depression of huge areas of London'. They also wished to eliminate the railway bridges across the Thames. These aims would be achieved by underground main-line railways, powered by clean electric motors, serving underground stations including Blackfriars, Charing Cross and Cannon Street which would be relocated beneath the surface and thus eliminate the need for the railway bridges across the Thames which served them.

MAIN-LINE TRAINS BENEATH LONDON

The idea of main-line trains running through large-diameter tunnels (a precursor of Crossrail) had already been proposed by a railwayman called George Dow in the London evening newspaper *The Star* on 14 June 1941. Dow proposed four new tunnels, each to accommodate main-line-gauge electric trains. They were: Paddington to Liverpool Street; Euston/King's Cross to Charing Cross – there would be a new station where these two lines crossed just to the North of Tottenham Court Road Underground station; Marylebone to Victoria; and Waterloo, south of the river, to Liverpool Street. All these lines would be linked to one another so that a passenger wishing to travel, for example, from Reading via Paddington or Southend via Liverpool Street to Brighton would be able to do so either by a direct service or by changing once, at a link station, without using the Tube.

The recommendations of Forshaw and Abercrombie were even more radical and were further explained in a commentary by the Modernist architect Erno Goldfinger (1902–87). The plan suggested

Blackfriars railway station and its bridge across the Thames would not have survived if the Abercrombie Report had been realised. The station would have gone underground, along with the one at Cannon Street, and the bridges would have been replaced by underground links. Having survived, they are now both major features of the Thameslink north–south service, which complements Crossrail's east–west line. (Sunil060902 via Wikimedia Commons CC SA 3.0)

that, in effect, the main-line termini north of the Thames should be linked by an underground suburban railway in a loop which would connect Paddington, Marylebone, Euston, King's Cross, Liverpool Street, Cannon Street, Blackfriars, Charing Cross, Victoria and back to Paddington: 'Suburban lines should be underground, linked with the tubes and kept separate from main line traffic.' There would also be a southern loop linking Cannon Street to London Bridge station, on to Waterloo and back beneath the river to Charing Cross, with further links to the Surrey Docks and Deptford. This plan, in all its ambition, could be described as 'Crossrail writ large'.

UNDERGROUND IN PLACE OF VIADUCTS

Forshaw and Abercrombie's plan would do away with the need for many surface terminals such as Cannon Street and Blackfriars and eliminate viaducts through built-up areas, particularly south of the Thames, which the authors found to be an intrusive source of noise and dirt. The underground ring, and other lines leading into London, would be electrified to reduce the dirt from steam (and later diesel) locomotives. The tunnels would be designed to accommodate main-line trains, with a reference to 'new facilities to take suitably equipped surface rolling stock'. A note of hesitancy crept into the report concerning the railways when the authors recommended that a 'special body' for railway planning be set up. Neither of the authors, Forshaw an architect and Abercrombie a town planner, had specialist knowledge of railways and it is as if, having recommended an ambitious and very expensive scheme to run main-line services beneath the surface of central London, they thought better of it and wondered whether it made sense. In a further radical recommendation they suggested that much of the 'Inner Circle [i.e. the existing Underground Circle Line] should become part of a ring to distribute goods from newly centralised markets'. This presumably referred to markets like Covent Garden, Billingsgate and Smithfield. Finally, those terminus stations which did survive on the surface (like Paddington, Euston and King's Cross) should have flat roofs suitable for use as 'aircraft landing grounds', since air transport was thought to have a future – so much for Brunel's glass roof at Paddington, soon to be listed! It should be noted that, despite the reference above to 'the possibilities of a duplication of tubes on certain lines', no mention was made of the idea of linking the deep shelters to give extra capacity for the Northern and Central Lines. They were forgotten in favour of the suburban ring and aircraft landing strips. The proposals could be described as ambitious!

The 'special body' proposed took the form of the Railway (London Plan) Committee which began work in 1944 and recommended no less than *ten* new routes, incorporating 102 miles of new tunnelling,

Old Billingsgate Market, along with other markets in central London, might have been served by deliveries from the Circle Line – a difficult idea to imagine. The old market has since been moved to Docklands, and the former market buildings are now occupied by financiers who probably do use the Circle Line to nearby Monument station. (Arild Vågen via Wikimedia Commons CC SA 3.0)

of which 39 miles were main-line-gauge tunnels of 17ft diameter, and 63 miles were Tube-gauge of 12ft diameter. Those were confident, expansive times, emboldened by wartime triumphs and ignorant of the privations of peace. Only one of the lines was ever built. It began life as 'Route C' and, after endless and frustrating delays (see below), opened as the Victoria Line in 1968. One proposal, Route F, hinted at a relief line for the Northern Line of the kind implied by the tunnel shelters but nothing came of it until, in modified form, it became the Jubilee Line in 1979.

Isambard Kingdom Brunel, the most famous and energetic of Victorian engineers. (Carlo Marochetti, by Tagishsimon via Wikimedia Commons CC SA 3.0)

Farringdon station, an early beneficiary of the development of the Thameslink service connecting the north and south of the Thames. (Mattbuck via Wikimedia Commons CC SA 3.0)

Canary Wharf (Ryan Tang on unsplash.com)

Canary Wharf roof garden, Crossrail Place, by Jason Williams. (Jayflux via Wikimedia Commons CC SA 4.0)

Crossrail Canary Wharf. (Tony Hisgett, via Wikimedia Commons CC 2.0)

Crossrail tunnel, December 2013. (Matt Brown via Wikimedia Commons CC 2.0)

Crossrail construction shaft, December 2013. (Matt Brown via WikimediaCommons CC 2.0)

Greenwich Crossrail TBM, May 2013. (DarkestElephant via Wikimedia Commons CC SA 3.0)

Removal of the temporary track at the Royal Oak Crossrail portal, London, prior to installation of overhead cable gantries and permanent track. (Marcus Rowland via WikimediaCommons CC SA 4.0)

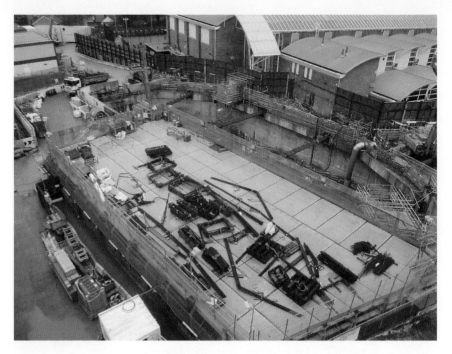

Whitechapel Crossrail work, December 2013. (Matt Brown via Wikimedia Commons CC 2.0)

A mock-up of the Crossrail rolling stock displayed at the London Transport Museum depot, Acton, prior to its production. (Frankie Roberto via Wikimedia Commons CC 2.0)

The first Class 345 Crossrail Line 1 (Elizabeth) train passes by platform 10a at Stratford station, London. Hauled by diesel locomotive 67 013 and with translator carriages at each end, this journey was taking the brand-new train to Ilford depot. (Spsmiler via Wikimedia Commons)

Class 345 unit 345007 interior, as of July 2017. (Sunil060902 via Wikimedia Commons CC SA 4.0)

Class 345 unit 345007 passes Stratford eastbound with an empty coaching stock service to Gidea Park sidings, on 7 July 2017. It had earlier arrived at Liverpool Street with the (at time of writing) daily westbound service from Shenfield. (Sunil060902 via Wikimedia Commons CC SA 4.0)

Class 345 unit 345007 passes Stratford eastbound with an empty coaching stock service to Gidea Park sidings, on 7 July 2017. It had earlier arrived at Liverpool Street with the (at time of writing) daily westbound service from Shenfield. (Sunil060902 via Wikimedia Commons CC SA 4.0)

SO WHERE'S THE MONEY!

If any of these plans had been adopted, the aims of the Abercrombie Report would have been achieved. Main-line services would have run beneath London from north to south and east to west, long pre-dating Crossrail, and the role of the Tube would have been largely short local journeys in the centre, more like buses than trains. In fact the plan, like much else, fell victim to the financial condition of the nation following the war. The achievements of the Attlee government, which in 1945 inherited a nation effectively bankrupted by the war, in creating the National Health Service, nationalising the worn out rail network and other industries and beginning the construction of housing to replace that destroyed by the war are extraordinary. But there were inevitably casualties and the railways, including the Underground, were prominent amongst them. The entire railway system, above and below ground, along with the inland waterways, road passenger and freight transport and the hotels formerly owned by the railways, were the responsibility of the British Transport Commission. This was an example of the idea that 'big government',

having won the war, would manage the peacetime economy equally effectively. But the Attlee government's priorities lay with hospitals and housing rather than transport, and the scarce capital resources available to the

Clement Attlee (1883–1967) with King George VI, after taking office as Prime Minister in 1945. His government's astonishing achievements in rebuilding a shattered nation after the war did not include much investment in the London railway network.

Treasury rarely found their way to the British Transport Commission. Moreover, the Underground was less severely damaged during the war and less run-down than the main-line railways which, running as they did on the surface, were more vulnerable to bomb damage. The main-line railways had to wait until 1955 and a Conservative government for the first Modernisation Plan and the Underground, even then, was still at the back of the queue for investment.

A FRUSTRATED CHAIRMAN

The Commission entrusted the management of the Underground to the London Transport Executive (LTE) while requiring it to submit to the Commission any proposal for capital expenditure exceeding £50,000. Even in 1948, the year the Executive was formed, that wasn't very much (the equivalent of little more than £1.5 million today) and was clearly inadequate to realise the ambitions of the County of London Plan. To put the figure into perspective, the Underground's New Works Programme of the 1930s had cost £30 million. And an examination of the LTE's accounts in the 1950s suggests that the Underground's assets were actually being run down in this period, with refurbished stations and the odd new escalator being largely financed by selling off land. The only capital expenditure of any consequence in the 1950s was the electrification of the Metropolitan Line north of Rickmansworth at a cost of £3.5 million, the last steam train running over this route in 1961. And this investment in the outer suburban network was, of course, contrary to the County of London's Plan, which had proposed investment in the central area rather than the commuter belt. In fact, the first significant investment in the Underground was the Victoria Line. First proposed in 1952 by a body of the kind recommended by the authors of the County of London Plan, it was subjected to endless delays despite the strong advocacy of Sir John Elliot, who had been appointed Chairman of the London Transport Executive in 1955. In the words of a Parliamentary Select Committee in 1965:

> By the end of the decade [1959] the Chairman [i.e. Sir John Elliot] was bang-
> ing the table and insisting that the work must be done. But as he had to work
> through the Commission the sound must have been muffled by the time
> it reached the Ministry. For this delay your Committee exonerate London
> Transport. They took every step within their power to press the scheme upon
> the authorities concerned.

This is rare praise for a nationalised undertaking from a group of
MPs. Eventually the government was persuaded to release the funds
for building the tunnels when the LTE said they would buy tunnel
segments from shipyards in the north-east of England, where the
government was worried about unemployment. Thus were decisions
made about Underground investment! In the circumstances it is not
surprising that the ambitious plans of Forshaw and Abercrombie for a
circle of main-line gauge trains with 'suitably equipped surface rolling
stock' in central London remained on paper.

Sir John Elliot (1898-1988) was the son of R.D. Blumenfeld,
editor of the *Daily Mail* and subsequently the *Daily Express*, who

changed his name to Elliot, his
mother's name, on the advice of
the newspaper proprietor Lord
Beaverbrook, who feared that
Blumenfeld's Jewish name would
provoke anti-Semitic sentiments.
The son followed his father into
journalism and became editor of

Sir Herbert Walker (1868–1949)
employed Elliot to promote the
services of the Southern Railway, and
Walker's establishment of a dense web
of electrified railways south of the
river helped to ensure that the London
Underground network in South
London was very limited compared to
that north of the river. (Elliot and Fry,
Railway magazine, July 1915)

IM TAKING AN EARLY HOLIDAY COS i KNOW SUMMER COMES SOONEST IN THE SOUTH
SOUTHERN RAILWAY

Sir John Elliot (1898–1988), after an early career in newspapers, created some very effective promotional posters for the Southern Railway before becoming the increasingly frustrated Chairman of the London Transport Executive. His formidable persuasive powers failed to persuade the Treasury to invest in what became, after many delays, the Victoria Line.

the *Evening Standard*, another Beaverbrook title. In 1925 Elliot joined the Southern Railway as public relations assistant to the chairman, Sir Herbert Walker, and produced some famous posters to promote the railway, like the one opposite. He rose to become General Manager of the Southern Railway. Following nationalisation of the network he became Chairman of the Railway Executive and, in 1953, Chairman of London Transport and a vigorous, often frustrated but eventually successful advocate of the Victoria Line though it did not open to passengers until 1968, nine years after he retired. He was knighted in 1954 for his services to the railway industry.

From the above it may be concluded that investment in the improvement of underground railway services of any kind in London in the post-war decades was very low indeed in the priorities of all the governments, Labour and Conservative, who held office. It was 1968 before the long-awaited Victoria Line took its first passengers.

SO WHAT HAPPENED TO THE DEEP SHELTERS?

As we have seen, the County of London Plan had no role for the deep shelters. There were no further proposals to link them to form an alternative or additional underground service to the crowded Northern or Central Lines. But they all found a use.

Goodge Street
The shelter at Goodge Street played a brief, heroic role in the Second World War. In 1942 it was used by General Eisenhower as his head-quarters for the initial planning of the invasion of Normandy before he moved to his advance headquarters at Southwick House near Portsmouth. For almost a year the area witnessed a procession of politicians, generals, admirals and air marshals as the plans for D-Day took shape. There was a direct connection by scrambler phone from the shelter to link Eisenhower and Churchill. After Eisenhower departed for Hampshire, three telephone lines were installed to link the shelter with the three D-Day beaches attacked by British and Canadian

The Chenies Street entrance to the Eisenhower deep-level shelter near Goodge Street Underground station. Once used to plan the invasion of Europe, it is now a document store. (Philafrenzy via Wikimedia Commons CC SA 4.0)

troops, Gold, Juno and Sword, and so on 6 June 1944 Goodge Street was the first to hear news of the fortunes of the troops as they fought their way ashore. As the armies advanced, Goodge Street's telephones followed them all the way to Berlin. The shelter, bedecked in vivid colours in Chenies Street, behind the British Museum, is now called the Eisenhower Centre and used as a store for archived documents. It has also featured in an episode of *Doctor Who*.

Clapham South

In 1948 the shelter at Clapham South station played a small part in English social history. When the *Empire Windrush*, with its 510 hopeful West Indian immigrants, approached Tilbury in 1948, the government wasn't sure what to do with them. Some of them had served in the forces during the war and their Commonwealth citizenship entitled them to enter the country. Eventually a former RAF policeman called Baron Baker was sent to welcome them and he conducted them to the Clapham South deep shelter as temporary accommodation. Many of them moved in and, in the days that followed, they sought and obtained employment at the Labour Exchange in nearby Brixton. Thus was born the Afro-Caribbean community of Brixton. In 1951 it became the Festival Hotel for visitors to the Festival of Britain and was later used for archival storage. It is now a Grade II listed building and can be visited on tours organised by the London Transport Museum in Covent Garden.

Clapham North

The Clapham North shelter long remained empty and neglected until, in 2006, Transport for London advertised its availability as a lease-hold property. Many expressed interest, with proposals for nightclubs and theme parks amongst the enquiries; even housing was suggested. However, considerations of safety in a 450m tunnel 33m beneath the streets ruled out many uses. Eventually it was taken over by the Zero Carbon Food Company which now uses hydroponic technology and low-energy artificial light to grow vegetables 33m beneath the streets. The Michelin starred chef Michel Roux was quoted as being 'blown away' by his visit to the site. It is anticipated that many of the 28,000kg of strawberries consumed at the Wimbledon tennis championships will be grown here, a few miles from the All-England Club.

Chancery Lane

The Chancery Lane shelter was used to store material from the Public Records Office between 1945 and 1949 when it was given to the General Post Office and used to house the Kingsway telephone exchange. It was also earmarked as a Cold War control centre. The exchange was closed in the 1980s when asbestos was found in the structure of the building.

Camden Town, Belsize Park, Stockwell, Clapham Common

These shelters, which are not open to the public, are used mostly for the archival storage of documents, video tapes and computer tapes, which evidently don't mind the cold, rather damp atmosphere which

Besides storing documents, the Stockwell shelter adds colour to its neighbourhood, as shown in this image by David Iliff, and is also a war memorial. (David Iliff via Wikimedia Commons CC SA 3.0)

prevails in them. The one near Stockwell station is strikingly decorated in bright cheerful colours as a First World War Memorial. Most of the shelters, including those never open to the public, have web entries posted by people who have visited them in the past and left descriptions and pictures of what they saw.

And so each of the shelters, built for Londoners as refuges from bombs, has found its place in London's history: document stores, accommodation for immigrants, visitors, the military, a telephone exchange or a novel means of producing food. But alas, the hope that they would contribute to solving London's transport problems was not to be realised. For that we have to look elsewhere.

5

ENTER CROSSRAIL

'The construction of two new railway lines in tunnels under central London.'

Central London Rail Study Report, 1989.

CROSSRAIL ENTERS THE DICTIONARY

The expression Crossrail was first used in the London Rail Study Report of 1974, prepared by the Department of the Environment (DoE) and the Greater London Council (GLC). It recommended a 'Crossrail' tunnel to link Paddington to the British Railways Eastern Region via Liverpool Street with intermediate stations at Marble Arch, Bond Street, Leicester Square and Holborn. It would be built to accommodate main-line-gauge rolling stock, which would have enabled passengers to travel east to west (and vice versa) across London without having to change trains or use the increasingly overburdened London Underground network: in effect, much of Crossrail but forty years early. It was applauded as imaginative and was compared in the report to the Paris RER (Reseau Express Regional) network, though the estimated cost of £300 million was a source of anxiety when the British economy, beset by strikes, was going through a particularly rough patch. It would also have required the electrification of main-line services on the Great Western line since diesel trains, with their fumes, would not have been tolerable underground. The services from Liverpool Street were already electrified by 1974. The Great Western is still awaiting electrification in 2018! A feasibility study was recommended but in the meantime 'safeguarding measures' were recommended to ensure that no development took place on the proposed route which would prevent or severely compromise any future proposals to build such a link. This prompted a number of property companies to start examining sites along the route in the belief that they would increase in value, especially if, as seemed at one time likely, the 'Crossrail' service was an express route like the Parisian RER rather than a stopping service as on the conventional Underground services.

THE FLEET LINE

The principal progeny of the study was the Fleet Line, eventually renamed the Jubilee Line. This had started life as Route F, the product of the 1944 London Plan Committee's ambitious proposals of which the Victoria Line (Route C) was the only other to see the light of day (see above). The original intention of the Fleet Line was that it should run beneath Fleet Street and below the valley of the River Fleet into the City via Ludgate Hill, thus relieving the overburdened Metropolitan, Northern and Bakerloo lines. This route was abandoned in favour of the present route. This begins at Stanmore in the north and passes, via the West End, beneath the Thames to Southwark and back across the Thames, via the new financial centre at Docklands and Canary Wharf, to Stratford in East London. So it still relieves the lines north of the capital but serves the 'New City' in Docklands rather than the old one in the Square Mile and goes nowhere near the River Fleet or the street that bears it name. In 1977, the year of the Queen's silver jubilee, the Conservatives, during the GLC elections, campaigned to change the name to the Jubilee Line. They won and the more appropriate name was adopted. The tunnel size is that of the other deep-level

The Fleet river is now a sewer beneath the Farringdon Road. Its name was destined to become that of a new Underground line, the Fleet Line, until a new route was chosen and the more dignified name Jubilee adopted. (Matt Brown from London via Wikimedia Commons CC 2.0)

Tubes (approximately 3.5m) but certain features mark it off from other lines – notably the platform screen doors in the Underground stations which reduce the level of noise associated with Underground trains and are an additional safety feature.

CENTRAL LONDON RAIL STUDY, 1989

Fifteen years passed before the government returned to the idea of a main-line railway beneath London, though in the 1980s British Rail kept the scheme alive with proposals for linking main-line railways to one another beneath London and hinting at links to Heathrow and to the still-distant prospect of the Channel Tunnel. The next major step was taken by Paul Channon, at the time Secretary of State for Transport in Margaret Thatcher's final government. The London economy was expanding rapidly following the reforms to the financial services sector in the 1980s. The City was booming and 'yuppies' with their extravagant coats, lifestyles and motor cars were eyeing the new developments in Docklands. Both road and rail systems within London were feeling the strain. In the words of Channon himself, in the preface to his report, which was issued in 1989:

> It was against this background that I set up the Central London Rail Study in March 1988. The Study has been conducted jointly between my Department, British Rail, London Regional Transport, and London Underground. A group under my Chairmanship, including the Chairmen of British Rail and London Regional Transport, has agreed that its findings should now be published.

The report called for a major upgrade of London's rail facilities and in particular for 'the construction of two new railway lines in tunnels under central London'. Cross London Rail Links (CLRL) was established as a partnership between Transport for London and Channon's Department of Transport to carry forward the Crossrail plan. At this stage it proposed a network of routes:

East-West Crossrail: Paddington to Marylebone and Liverpool Street (as proposed in 1974) with intermediate stations at Tottenham Court Road and Bond Street; cost £885 million.

City Crossrail: from London Bridge to Essex Road with intermediate stations at Fenchurch Street and Liverpool Street. Essex Road is on the Great Northern Line north of King's Cross; cost £520 million.

North–South Crossrail: linking the West Coast main line from Euston to Victoria via Stations at Tottenham Court Road and Piccadilly Circus; cost £895 million.

A Chelsea–Hackney Line was also suggested in conjunction with the East–West Crossrail link, and although it was not pursued at the time it has been earmarked as a route for Crossrail 2 (see chapter 11). There was also a proposal to upgrade the Thameslink Metro Service between King's Cross and Blackfriars and then across the Thames to the south at a cost of £330 million. This link has been steadily expanded over the years and now connects Bedford with Kent and Sussex via St Pancras, and Cambridge and Peterborough with the same destinations via King's Cross and St Pancras.

In 2004 a more ambitious plan was put forward by a group of experienced senior railway managers. They proposed a network embracing Reading, Northampton, Cambridge, Ipswich, Southend, Guildford and Basingstoke – the area to the south and south-east of London being excluded presumably because of the dense network of lines created there between the wars by Sir Herbert Walker's Southern Railway. Cross London Rail Links considered the proposal but concluded that the improvement in longer-distance services would make it much more difficult to meet the real need, which was that of providing more frequent services in the central area. The Crossrail scheme, now without serious rivals, set out on its long, slow and often frustrating journey through the legislative process.

THE FIRST CROSSRAIL BILL

In November 1991 a Bill was submitted to Parliament by London Underground and British Rail that reflected the hopes of the study and estimated the cost at a little over £2 billion at 1993 prices. It fell foul of the recession of the early 1990s and the Thatcher government's view that such projects should be funded by the beneficiaries: the fare-paying passengers and the property owners and developers who would benefit from the scheme. In the conditions of the 1990s property developers were not in an expansive mood and in 1994 Parliament rejected the Bill at the Select Committee stage. Further delays followed as governments tried, without success, to find cheaper or more cost-effective alternatives and dithered over whether public money should be committed to the project. In the meantime the process of safeguarding the route continued while property developers, still alive to the possible profits to be made

Hemel Hempstead was a quiet little village before it became, along with Stevenage and others, a post-war 'new town', absorbing the Londoners whose homes had been destroyed in the Blitz. The capital's population fell by almost 2 million but by 2015 it had recovered to its pre-war level, putting greater demands on the transport system and strengthening the case for Crossrail.

from enhanced values along the route, continued to identify possible sites for purchase and development. It seems very likely that they will be rewarded. It is estimated that by 2021 over £5 billion will have been added to the value of property along the Crossrail route. By the year 2000 the Labour government's transport strategy was supporting the idea of an East–West link beneath London, and the Labour Mayor, Ken Livingstone, was drawing attention to the chronic overcrowding on the London Underground. In 2002 Cross London Rail Links was given a budget of £154 million to prepare and present a business case.

By this time an additional factor had entered the debate on the side of those who were advocating better rail services to and within the capital: the population of London, after a long post-war decline, was beginning to grow. As the war began in 1939 London's population reached a historic peak of 8.6 million. The devastation of war, particularly the relentless bombing in its early phases, led to the demolition of many slums in the 1940s and 1950s and the movement of much of the population to the 'new towns', such as Hemel Hempstead and Stevenage. These changes led to a new emphasis on commuter services for those who, while still working in London, were living in these new communities several miles distant. By 1981 the population of the capital had fallen to 6.8 million but thereafter it began a slow recovery so that, by 2015, it reached the pre-war total with all that implied for the need for better transport within the capital.

THE CROSSRAIL BILL 2008

In February 2005 another Crossrail Bill was presented to Parliament and by this time it had been accepted that public investment in the scheme was justified. The preamble of the Bill makes its purpose clear:

> A Bill to make provision for a railway transport system running from Maidenhead in the county of Berkshire, and Heathrow Airport, in the London Borough of Hillingdon, through London to Shenfield, in the County of Essex and Abbey Wood, in the London Borough of Greenwich, and for connected purposes.

After three further years of debate and scrutiny, the project that received Royal Assent in July 2008 was clearly a descendant of the schemes of Isambard Kingdom Brunel, Charles Pearson, the Regents Canal Company and the Abercrombie Plan. It would be an East–West route of main-line gauge, free of smoke (thanks to electricity), beginning at Maidenhead (later amended to Reading) and Heathrow in the west and passing to Shenfield and Abbey Wood in the east and south-east. During the debates on the Bill it was suggested that an additional station be added at Woolwich, a request that was eventually accepted by the sponsors, the Department for Transport and Transport for London. It would be financed, to the tune of approximately £15 billion, by government, Transport for London and the private sector in the form of the owners of Heathrow airport and the City of London, with a loan of £1 billion from the European Investment Bank. And so the digging could begin at last.

6

NEW TECHNOLOGY: TUNNELLING SHIELDS AND ELECTRICITY

'The conductor was all of a quiver of joy and pride. But there was no indecorous exhibition of emotion: every man was solidly British.'

The *Daily Mail* on the opening of the Central London Railway, later the Central Line, 1900.

BETTER SHIELDS

The tunnelling shield of Marc Brunel had, after eighteen years and many misadventures, succeeded in completing the Thames Tunnel, as explained in chapter 1. In the decades that followed, advances were made in shield design and equipment that made it possible to construct the deep-level tubes, the Channel Tunnel, the Thames Tideway Relief Sewer and, eventually, the Crossrail tunnels. The first advance was made by a civil engineer called Peter William Barlow (1809–85) who, in 1862, had sunk cast-iron cylinders into the Thames to support a suspension bridge at Lambeth (replaced by the present arch bridge in 1932). Barlow had concluded that if the cylinders were turned on their sides they could form a tunnel beneath the river that would be easier, safer and cheaper to construct than Marc Brunel's tunnel of brick. He conceived the idea of building another tunnel beneath the Thames, close to the later site of Tower Bridge, but when he tried to find contractors to do the construction work he discovered that they were all deterred by the problems encountered by Marc Brunel. He patented a design for a cylindrical shield with cutting plates at its head and this, with modifications, was used by a pupil of Barlow's, a South African engineer called James Henry Greathead (1844–96), who had come to England in 1859, to build the Tower Subway. This still runs beneath the Thames from Tower Hill to a site close to the present site of HMS *Belfast*. Barlow's shield was 2.2m in diameter, slightly larger than the 2.06m prefabricated iron tunnel cylinders which were bolted into place as the shield advanced. Liquid cement

The entrance to the Tower Subway, near the Tower of London, along which passenger carriages were hauled by a cable across the Thames from 1870. The subway did not survive the opening of Tower Bridge but is still a conduit for pipes and cables beneath the river. (Phillip Perry via Wikimedia Commons CC 2.0)

A Tower Subway carriage drawing passengers across the Thames between Tower Hill and Vine Lane, off Tooley Street, on the South Bank.

was then forced through holes in the segments to secure them firmly to the outer ring of London clay. The tunnel, 450m long, was bored in less than a year compared with the eighteen years taken by the Brunels for the 396m Thames Tunnel. The Tower Subway started life in 1870 as a narrow-gauge railway whose carriages were drawn across the river by cable, at a fare of twopence first class and a penny second class, the power being provided by a stationary steam engine at either end. The railway did not long survive the opening of Tower Bridge but still exists as a means of conducting water and power lines beneath the river.

THE FIRST TUBE: THE CITY & SOUTH LONDON RAILWAY

The first deep-level tube proposed was the City & South London Railway between King William Street, a station now closed on the north side of London Bridge, and Elephant & Castle, a mile to the south. It would have been little more than a river crossing, but as its possibilities became clearer it was extended to Stockwell in South London, a distance of 3½ miles. The tunnelling shield for this venture was similar to that designed by Greathead. He adopted the cylindrical design used on the Tower subway but in addition to the tunnelling 'miners' employed by Brunel and Barlow, he equipped his shield with sharp steel blades, which were forced into the clay by powerful hydraulic rams applying a pressure of 1 ton per sq.in.

Miners then excavated the loosened clay and loaded it on to wagons on rails, which were drawn away by ponies. The first shaft was sunk close to the north end of London Bridge in 1889 and tunnels of just over 3m in diameter were driven north to the first terminus at King William Street and south, beneath the river, to Stockwell. The tunnels

The statue of James Greathead (1844–96) outside Bank Underground station. The station, on the Central and Northern Lines, owes its existence to the fact that Greathead's development of tunnelling shield technology enabled those lines to be created. (JustinC via Wikimedia Commons 2.0)

THE WATERLOO AND CITY ELECTRICAL UNDERGROUND RAILWAY

MINERS AT WORK IN THE SHIELD AT THE FACE　　FILLING BETWEEN RIBS AND SURFACING THE IRON TUNNEL WITH CONCRETE

A Greathead shield being used to build the Waterloo & City Line. It is similar to that used to build the City & South London Railway. Sharp blades at the head of the shield help the miners to do their work. (James C. Cole)

were more than 12m beneath the surface, well below sewers and foundations, and, like the Metropolitan Railway, followed the line of the streets to avoid claims for damage from property owners.

ELECTRICITY UNDERGROUND

The City& South London Railway (now, with enlarged tunnels, part of the Northern Line) opened to the public in December 1890, the official opening having been performed the previous month, amongst much celebration, by the Prince of Wales. The line was also the first to use electric locomotives, which were essential given the depth beneath the surface, and this form of traction was to be the future of underground railway operation. The original plan had been for the line to use a cable system as a form of propulsion, like that of the Tower Subway. A stationary steam engine would pull a continuous cable from which trains would be detached as they reached stations and to which they would be reattached as they left.

Presumably the journey would have been rather jerky. As the railway advanced from the originally planned terminus at Elephant & Castle to Stockwell, with additional stops at Borough, Kennington, Oval (and later London Bridge) and round many bends, the cable became less feasible; so, with commendable boldness, the directors decided to adopt the novel, and far from proven, system of electric traction. In 1879 Werner von Siemens had exhibited a small electric locomotive at the Berlin Trade Fair and in 1883 his compatriot, Magnus Volk, constructed a small electric railway on the Brighton seafront where it still provides rides for passengers. After consulting many engineers (including the ubiquitous John Fowler who charged the typically outrageous fee of £2,500 for his services) the

The former site of the original terminus of the City & South London Railway, now the Northern Line, is marked by a blue plaque. The station was soon replaced by Bank station and the site is occupied by Regis House on the northern end of London Bridge. The station itself remains in use as a document store. (Spudgun67 via Wikimedia Commons CC SA 4.0)

directors asked the Manchester firm of Mather and Platt to electrify the line. Sir William Mather had secured the rights to manufacture Thomas Edison's dynamo in Britain and employed two brilliant scientists from Cambridge, the brothers John and Edward Hopkinson, to make improvements to Edison's design.

Werner Von Siemens's locomotive at the Berlin trade fair in 1883 began to realise some of the possibilities revealed by the work of Michael Faraday and made possible the operation of the Tube railways by electric traction. He later gave his name to one of the world's greatest companies. (Photograph by Giacomo Brogi (1822–81))

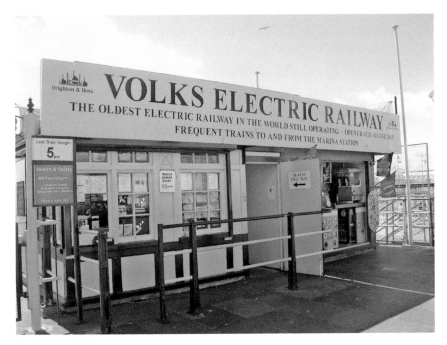

Magnus Volk's electric railway is still bearing his name and carrying passengers along Brighton seafront more than a century later. (Briantist via Wikimedia Commons CC SA 2.5)

ELECTRICITY!

They built a power station at the Stockwell terminus, using Edison–Hopkinson dynamos, and used an electric locomotive, which ran at 25 miles per hour on 450 volts of current. Each train consisted of three wooden carriages, seating thirty-two passengers and known as 'padded cells'. They had very comfortable seats but were narrow since the tunnels were only 3.1m in diameter, with slits for windows, just above head height. The carriages were lit by electricity. *Punch* called them sardine boxes. Both the locomotives and the 'padded cell' carriages may be seen at London's Transport Museum in Covent Garden. The fare, for any distance travelled, was twopence, with no distinction between first- and second-class passengers. This greatly worried the editor of *The Railway Times*, who deplored the innovation: 'We have scarcely yet been educated up to that condition of social equality when lords and ladies will be content to ride side by side with Billingsgate "fish fags" and Smithfield porters.' This did not deter the 5,161,398 passengers who used the service in its first year.

Far more interest was shown in the novel electric traction. The Prince of Wales was presented with a golden key when he switched on the current and *The Illustrated London News* explained at length, with pictures and diagrams, how electricity was generated and how it was transmitted to the motors that turned the wheels. There were to be some anxious moments. As the railway passed beneath the Thames it entered a dip from which it emerged as it reached the riverbank and the stations at King William Street and Borough. When the train was fully loaded, the little locomotives, now far from the power station at Stockwell, sometimes struggled up the incline, lights flickering. On occasions the train would have to reverse and take another 'run' at it. Nevertheless, despite these anxieties it was a glimpse of the future that would transform travel beneath the streets of London.

Thomas Edison. His dynamo, manufactured under licence by William Mather and improved by the Hopkinson brothers, provided the power to drive the little locomotives of the City & South London Railway. (Library of Congress)

ELECTRIC RAILWAY TRAIN.

City & South London Railway carriages were known as 'padded cells' on account of their tiny windows and lavish upholstery. Scandal arose in some quarters at the abolition of classes so that the gentry had to sit with 'Billingsgate fish fags'!

'LONDON WILL BECOME QUITE A NICE PLACE TO TRAVEL IN'

The next major development in the tube system was the official opening of the Central London Railway (the Central Line) in June 1900, running initially from Bank (then called Cornhill) to Shepherd's Bush. The ceremony was performed once again by the Prince of Wales in the presence of a number of VIPs including the American Samuel Clemens, better known as Mark Twain. The importance of the occasion was reflected not only in its opening by royalty (a feature of Underground travel which continues in the reign of Elizabeth II) but in the excitement of the press. The *Daily Mail* wrote of:

> … voracious curiosity, astonished satisfaction and solid merit … if this kind of thing goes on London will become quite a nice place to travel in … the conductor was all of a quiver of joy and pride. But there was no indecorous exhibition of emotion: every man was solidly British.

As on the City & South London Railway, a flat fare of twopence was adopted. There was, too, no distinction between first and second class. This became a feature of Underground travel, though it has been abandoned in the case of Crossrail.

Electric traction, like single-class travel, remained a feature of the new railway but with new, more powerful American locomotives, whose great weight and crude suspension caused such vibrations that draughtsmen in Cheapside offices complained that they were unable to draw straight lines on diagrams. The tunnels had been begun in 1896 under the direction of three distinguished engineers: Benjamin Baker, designer of the Forth Bridge; James Greathead; and the ever-present John Fowler, who died in 1898 but no doubt received a generous share of the fee of £93,000 paid to the trio. Greathead shields were used, as on the City & South London tunnels, though the tunnels were on a larger gauge than the City & South London's with a diameter of 3.5m, which was to become the standard size for deep-level tubes.

Mark Twain, whose presence at the opening of the Central London Railway in 1900 added some lustre to the occasion.

THE PRICE ROTARY EXCAVATOR

But the days of the Greathead shields were numbered. In 1900 an American, Charles Tyson Yerkes, led a syndicate which bought the right to construct the Charing Cross, Euston & Hampstead Railway (now the northern branch of the Northern Line). The syndicate engaged the contractors Price and Reeves to undertake the tunnelling. In its relatively short life (1897–1927) the company was involved in two major projects for which it deserves to be remembered: the Rotherhithe Tunnel, which opened in 1908 and the Charing Cross, Euston & Hampstead railway, which entered service in 1907. But the railway was notable for the fact that, for the first time, it made use of a new type of tunnelling shield, Price's rotary excavator, designed by the eponymous John Price, which marked a further step forward in tunnelling technology. As well as having blades which projected forwards and broke the ground ahead of them, like Greathead's, Price's shield incorporated electrically powered angled rotating knives at the head of the shield, which cut into the surface and pushed the excavated material to the rear from which it could be carried away by conveyor belt or wagon. This enabled tunnels to be driven forward at unprecedented speed through the predominant London clay, though for more difficult, marshy ground Greathead shields were still used as late as the 1960s for the construction of the Victoria Line. This was to be the model for future tunnelling technology.

TUNNELLING: EIGHT RESOLUTE WOMEN

When the Channel Tunnel was built, between 1988 and 1994, eleven tunnel-boring machines (TBM) were used, working from both sides of the channel. The English machines were identified with letters and numbers but the French TBMs, showing a little more flair, were given the names of women: *Brigitte, Europa, Catherine, Virginie, Pascaline* and *Séverine*. This tradition has been adopted by Crossrail, with the hope that it will make it clear that women are welcome in the engineering profession. Since some of the principal engineers on the project have been women, perhaps it worked. Following a public vote on February 2012 Crossrail announced the names of six of the machines the following month, with two others added following the 2012 London Olympic Games. The names were as follows, with a brief description of the ladies after whom they were named:

Ada and Phyllis

Augusta Ada King-Noel, Countess of Lovelace (1815–52), computer pioneer, was the only legitimate child of the Romantic poet Lord Byron and his wife Anne Milbanke. Byron deserted Ada's mother a month after Ada was born, left England for ever four months later and had no further contact with his daughter, despite which Ada remained loyal to Byron. An early (and for a woman of that time uncharacteristic) interest in mathematics and logic was encouraged by her mother, possibly as a perceived antidote to the reckless behaviour and perceived insanity of Byron himself. As a young woman, and with her mother's encouragement, she met Charles Dickens and the scientist Michael Faraday. More significantly, through an introduction

by her personal tutor Mary Somerville she met the mathematician Charles Babbage, with whom she worked on his Analytical Engine, an idea for an early mechanical computer. Mary Somerville, herself a Mathematician, later gave

Ada Lovelace (1815–52), Byron's neglected, faithful and very gifted daughter, was one of the pioneers of computing and is remembered in the tunnelling machine that bears her name. (Stipple engraving, based on a drawing by Frank Stone)

her name to Somerville College, Oxford. Between 1842 and 1843, Ada translated an article by Italian military engineer Luigi Menabrea together with notes which resemble a simple computer programme. In 1835 she married William King, who in 1838 became Earl of Lovelace, Ada thereby becoming Countess of Lovelace. She died in 1852 aged 36, after a lifetime of ill health, and was, at her own request, buried close to her neglectful father, Byron, in the churchyard of St Mary Magdalene, Hucknall, Nottinghamshire. Along with Babbage she is regarded as one of the pioneers of computing.

Phyllis Pearsall (1906–96), designer of the *London A–Z*, was born Phyllis Gross in East Dulwich, the daughter of a Hungarian Jewish immigrant, Alexander Grosz (changed to Gross) and Isabella Crowley, a suffragette of Irish-Italian descent. Her father founded the Geographia cartographic company, which produced street maps of British towns, but went bankrupt, following which Phyllis had to leave Roedean school. Phyllis later visited Paris where she studied at the Sorbonne and met the writer Vladimir Nabokov. Her brother was the artist Anthony Gross, an artist who attended the Slade School and later, as a war artist, landed in France with the British troops on D-Day, 6 June 1944. She married an artist friend of her brother, Richard Pearsall, from whom she separated after eight years of marriage. By 1935 she was a portrait painter in London. Having on occasion become lost in London, Phyllis decided to follow her father's example in cartography by producing a comprehensive street plan of London which, for the first time, included many house numbers. Her working day began at 5 a.m. and was followed by an eighteen hour day, eventually walking an estimated 3,000 miles checking the names and layout of London's 23,000 streets. The maps were drawn by her father's cartographer using the 6in Ordnance Survey maps of London. In 1936 she printed 10,000 copies of the completed maps and, after being rejected by the main London booksellers, including Foyle's, Hatchards and Selfridges, she secured an order from W.H. Smith, which was swiftly followed by orders from Woolworths and others. Her *London A–Z* became a mainstay of London station bookstalls. Until her father's death in 1958, copies of the book included the accreditation 'Produced under the direction of Alexander Gross, FRGS'. (Fellow of the Royal Geographical Society). Nevertheless her father's contribution to the work was modest. In 1986 she was awarded the MBE and in 1990 she wrote an account of her life and work called *From Bedsitter to Household Name*. In 2005 Southwark Council installed a blue plaque on the house where she was born in Court Lane Gardens, Dulwich.

Sophia and Mary

Sophia Kingdom (1775–1855) was born in Plymouth, the youngest of sixteen children of William Kingdom, a contractor for the Royal Navy and the British Army. Her father died when she was 8 years old and she was sent to France as a governess to improve her knowledge of the language. In the early years of the French Revolution she met Marc Brunel while they were both working in Rouen. Marc, a royalist, fled to the United States in 1793 during the reign of terror, leaving Sophia in France to be arrested as a suspected English spy with every expectation that she would be executed. Marc returned from the United States in 1799 after an absence of six years and began to search for Sophia, learning that she had left France in 1795 following the fall of Robespierre. They were reunited and married in November 1799. They had two daughters, Sophia and Emma, their third child being the famous engineer Isambard Kingdom Brunel, his middle name being that of his mother's family. In 1841, after her adventure accompanying her son Isambard in the diving bell (see chapter 1) she became Lady Brunel when Marc was knighted by Queen Victoria. Like her daughter-in-law Mary, Sophia spent many years of a happy marriage as an 'engineering widow', as her husband Marc, like their son, devoted his waking hours to ingenious and innovatory but time-consuming engineering projects. She died in 1855 and was buried in the family grave in Kensal Green cemetery with her husband and son.

Mary Horsley Brunel (1813–81) was the wife of the celebrated engineer Isambard Kingdom Brunel (1803-59) whom she married in 1836, establishing a home in Duke Street, St James. The marriage produced three children, one of whom, Henry Brunel, became a well-known civil engineer who worked on the designs for Blackfriars Railway Bridge and Tower Bridge. Mary was born Mary Horsley, and came from a distinguished musical family, her father William Horsley being an organist and composer who composed the tune to the Easter hymn 'There is a Green Hill Far Away'. The tune bears the composer's name, and he composed another popular tune, 'Belgrave', to the hymn 'When all Thy mercies, O my God, My rising soul surveys'. Mary's father was a friend of the composer Mendelssohn, and Mary and her family were, it is claimed, the first to hear Mendelssohn play, on their family piano, his music for *A Midsummer Night's Dream*. She married Isambard when he was resident engineer for the Thames Tunnel

The Brunel family tomb at Kensal Green contains the graves of Marc and his wife Sophia, his son Isambard and his wife Mary. The wives gave their names to two of the TBMs creating Crossrail. (Threefoursixninefour via Wkimedia Commons CC 3.0)

designed by Isambard's father Marc, whose tribulations are described in chapter 1, and when Mary's new husband was in daily peril of death by tunnel collapse or drowning. Once the tunnel was completed Mary had to endure Isambard's frequent long absences on his projects, including the Great Western Railway and the designing of the Clifton Suspension Bridge, which was completed after his death. She also had to cope with incidents arising from his high spirits, as when, in 1843, while performing a conjuring trick for his children, Isambard accidentally inhaled a half-sovereign, which became locked in his windpipe. For several days it was the talk of London clubs, with members greeting one another with the question 'Is it out?' until it was eventually expelled after the patient was strapped upside down to a board and shaken vigorously. Such were the ordeals of an engineering widow! He convalesced at Teignmouth and was so taken with the area that he purchased an estate at Watcombe, near Torquay, where Brunel Manor was built, though the couple never lived there as Isambard died in 1859 before it was completed. Mary died in 1881 after a long widowhood and was buried in the family grave in Kensal Green cemetery with her husband.

Victoria and Elizabeth

These ladies hardly need to be introduced but their relevance to the Crossrail project perhaps deserves some words of explanation.

Queen Victoria's reign, from 1837–1901 coincided with the great engineering achievements of the nineteenth century including the completion of the Thames Tunnel in 1843 by Marc Brunel and the construction of much of the railway network, most notably of the London Underground. Victoria was, of course, the world's first monarch to travel by train. On 13 June 1842 the queen travelled with Prince Albert on the Great Western Railway from Slough to Paddington, driven by Isambard Kingdom Brunel accompanied by Daniel Gooch who actually designed the locomotive. A luxurious royal saloon had been provided by the Great Western Railway (GWR) in anticipation of the occasion (the first royal train) in which, according to *The Times*, 'fittings are upon a most elegant and magnificent scale, tastefully improved by bouquets of rare flowers arranged within the carriage'. The 18-mile journey took twenty-five minutes at an average speed of 43 miles per hour. Brunel and Gooch may have been carried away by the occasion since it seems that the queen found the speed excessive. The GWR later fitted a signal by which the queen's attendants could ask the driver to slow down.

The present Queen's reign, of course, has seen an expansion in the Underground system greater than any since the early years of the twentieth century. She officially opened the Victoria Line in March 1969, named after her great-great-grandmother, and saw the opening of the Jubilee Line in 1979, named for her own silver jubilee two years previously. She also opened the Docklands Light Railway in 1977 and has now seen the birth of Crossrail, which will be named the Elizabeth Line in her honour upon entering service in autumn 2019.

Jessica and Ellie

Following the London Olympics, a further consultation was launched for names for the last two TBMs, the names being those of 'modern heroes'. The names chosen were suggested by Marion Richardson primary School in Stepney Green, east London.

Jessica Ennis-Hill, athlete, was born in 1986 in Sheffield, the daughter of a father of Jamaican descent who worked as a self-employed painter and decorator and an English mother who was a social worker. Her parents introduced her to athletics at Sheffield's Don Valley Stadium because, as Jessica later joked, 'I think my mum and dad wanted me out of the house.' At school Jessica distinguished herself both in the classroom and on the sports field, gaining a degree in psychology at Sheffield University and starting to win at national sprint and high jump events in 2004 aged 18. She won bronze in the heptathlon at the 2006 Commonwealth Games in Melbourne and finished fourth in the heptathlon at the 2007 World Championships in Japan. Despite injury setbacks in 2008, she won gold at the Berlin

World Championships in Berlin the following year. European gold followed in 2010, a second world title in 2011 (following disqualification, after a drugs test, of the original 'winner') and in 2012 she achieved lasting fame at the London Olympics on 'Super Saturday' when, following one cycling and two rowing gold medals, Jessica won gold in the Olympic stadium in the heptathlon, the roar of the 80,000-strong crowd as she took the lead in the final of the 800m threatening to bring down the stadium walls. Greg Rutherford and Mo Farah also won gold medals that day. Other more unusual distinctions followed. She was featured on a Royal Mail postage stamp and on the front page of *The Beano* as Ennis the Menace, and a postbox in Sheffield was painted gold in her honour. In May 2013 she married Andy Hill and has been known since that time as Jessica Ennis-Hill. She gave birth to son Reggie in 2014, won a silver medal in the Rio Olympics in 2016 and gave birth to daughter Olivia in 2017, becoming Dame Jessica Ennis-Hill in the New Year Honours of that year.

The London Olympic stadium nears completion in 2011 and awaits the arrival of Jessica Ennis, Ellie Simmonds and many others for the opening ceremonies of the games. (EG Focus via Wikimedia Commons CC 2.0)

Ellie Simmonds, a paralympian swimmer, was born in 1994 in Walsall and has the condition known as Achondroplasia, a common cause of dwarfism, shortness of stature. A keen swimmer from the age of 5, she moved to Swansea when she was 11 to take advantage of the excellent swimming and coaching facilities available in that city. She achieved national recognition when she won two gold medals at the 2008 Summer Paralympics in Beijing, where she was the youngest member of the team, aged 13. In 2012 at the London Olympics she won two further gold medals as well as a silver and a bronze medal, setting a world record in the 400m freestyle event. In her honour two postboxes were painted gold: one in Walsall where she was born and one in Swansea. Another gold (and world record) followed in the 200m medley event at Rio, together with a further bronze. In 2008 Ellie was voted the BBC Young Sports Personality of the Year and in the New Year Honours of 2009 she was made MBE. An OBE followed in 2013 for services to Paralympic sport.

7

MOBILE FACTORIES TUNNELLING BENEATH LONDON

'Open-heart surgery on a patient while the patient is alive.'

A description of the process of building Crossrail beneath central London

London is no stranger to tunnels. When engineers were invited to tender for the work of creating the new Crossrail route beneath central London they were aware of the network of tunnels which already ran beneath the capital and through which they would have to thread a new tunnel with a diameter of 6.2m.

TUNNELS BENEATH LONDON

The maze of tunnels beneath the capital comes in all shapes and sizes. Some of the more historic are listed below, in date order:

The Thames Tunnel	1843	396m
The intercepting sewers of Sir Joseph Bazalgette	1859–75	131km
Metropolitan Railway	1863	6km
The Tower Subway	1870	450m
City & South London Railway	1890	5.1km
Blackwall Tunnel	1897	1.35km
Great Northern, Piccadilly & Brompton Railway (the Piccadilly Line)	1906	9.1km
Rotherhithe Tunnel	1908	1.4km
Post Office Railway	1927	10.5km
Deep shelters	1942	3.7km
Victoria Line	1969	21km
Jubilee Line	1979	36.2km
Crossrail	2018	42km

(For comparison, the Channel Tunnel, 50km long, entered service in 1994, having been constructed in six years, beginning in 1988.)

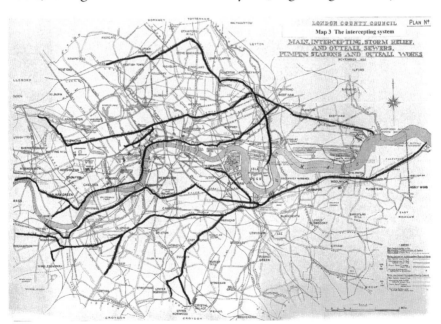

Sir Joseph Bazalgette's sewer network, seen on this map, is only one of the obstacles that Crossrail had to navigate in its tunnelling work. (Courtesy of Thames Water plc)

This main sewer, in east London, is one of the larger obstacles that the Crossrail line in nearby Whitechapel had to avoid. (Courtesy of Thames Water plc)

The Porchester is a popular pub on the site of the former Royal Oak, close to where the Crossrail line enters the tunnel that takes it beneath central London. (Tom Morris via Wikimedia Commons CC SA 3.0)

In August 2009 invitations to tender for the tunnelling work were published in the *Official Journal of the European Union* and towards the end of 2010 the contracts were awarded to seven companies. Tunnelling began on 4 May 2012, when *Phyllis* set out from Royal Oak portal, to the west of Paddington, to her destination at Farringdon, shortly followed by *Ada*, driving the parallel tunnel in the same direction. Portals are the entry points at which the tunnelling machines can begin their work of creating the tunnels. They are situated at:

Royal Oak, west of Paddington; takes its name from an eighteenth-century tavern whose site is now occupied by a pub called The Porchester at 88 Bishop's Bridge Road. *Phyllis* began work in May 2012, shortly joined by *Ada* on their journey to Farringdon. Boris Johnson, Mayor of London and Justine Greening, Transport Secretary, were there to bid *Phyllis* farewell as she set out on her 6.8km journey to Farringdon.

Pudding Mill Lane, E16, near the Olympic Park and the Docklands Light Railway station of that name, where *Jessica* and *Ellie* set out for Stepney Green in August 2013 and February 2014 respectively.

Plumstead, in the London Borough of Greenwich where *Sophia* and *Mary* set out for North Woolwich in January and May 2013 respectively.

North Woolwich, on the north bank of the Thames, south of London City Airport and close to North Woolwich station on the Docklands Light Railway where *Sophia* and *Mary* emerged a year after they enter the tunnel at Plumstead.

Victoria Dock in the London Borough of Newham, close to Royal Victoria station on the Docklands Light Railway, from which *Jessica* and *Ellie* emerged after tunnelling from the Limmo peninsula, Canning Town, to which they had been transported by road once they had finished their first task of tunnelling from Pudding Mill Lane to Stepney Green.

Pudding Mill Lane station, on the Docklands Light Railway, now shares its curious name with one of the portals through which Crossrail enters its tunnel to cross London from east to west. (Sunil060902 via Wikimedia Commons CC SA 3.0)

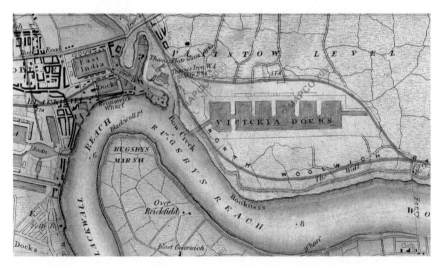

This map of 1872 of the Victoria Dock gives a good idea of the marshy terrain through which *Jessica* and *Ellie* had to tunnel from the Limmo Peninsula, which is the thin strip of land to the north-west. Bugsby's marsh, on the south of the river, to the left of the picture, is the present site of the Millennium Dome. (*Wyld's New Topographical Map Of The Country In The Vicinity Of London c.* 1872.)

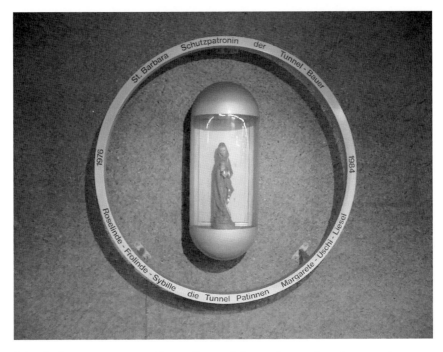

Saint Barbara, patron saint of tunnellers and those who work underground, was placed in the tunnels while work proceeded. In this picture, appropriately, she watches proceedings in an underground station in Frankfurt. (Michael König via Wikimedia Commons CC SA 3.0)

It was at the Limmo Peninsula that *Victoria* and *Elizabeth* joined the tunnelling team when they were lowered by crane into the shaft created for the purpose on 25 October 2012 before setting out for Farringdon, which they reached in May 2015, to mark the end of tunnelling.

A statue of St Barbara, a third-century Greek martyr and patron saint of tunnellers, miners and workers concerned with explosives, was placed in the tunnels while work proceeded.

MOBILE FACTORIES

Each of the tunnelling machines is, in effect, a mobile factory. All eight machines were designed and manufactured by the German company Herrenknecht, based in Schwanau, Baden-Wurttemberg since,

The cutting face of TBM *Ada*; she is about to be moved into place to begin her journey from the Royal Oak portal, near Paddington, to Farringdon in May 2012. Transported to the location by road on a low loader, *Ada* is waiting for a footbridge to be raised so that she can pass beneath it. The remainder of her apparatus will then be connected to her so that she can begin work. (Marcus Rowland via Wikimedia Commons)

This photograph gives an impression of the equipment behind the cutting face, which processes and removes the material extracted by *Ada* from the tunnel at Royal Oak. (Marcus Rowland via Wikimedia Commons)

ironically, there are no longer any British manufacturers to continue the work of Marc Brunel, James Greathead and John Price. The first components for *Phyllis* and *Ada* were delivered to Westbourne Park, west of Paddington and close to Royal Oak, the point where they were to be used. There the TBMs were assembled from approximately fifty components shipped from Germany. Each tunnelling machine worked round the clock manned by a twenty-man crew for each shift, twelve of them on the machine itself and the remainder working to the rear, supervising the disposal of excavated material and the installation of the concrete rings which formed the tunnel lining. Each TBM costs approximately £11 million, weighs approximately 1,000 tons, is 147m long and headed by a cutting wheel made of tungsten carbide, which is forced against the cutting face by hydraulic pressure. Behind the cutting head is a screw conveyor that takes the excavated material to a conveyor belt, which moves the material out of the tunnel. The TBMs are 7.1m in diameter which enables them to cut a tunnel of 6.2m, allowing for the insertion of concrete tunnel lining segments

The teeth on the cutting face that *Sophia* and *Mary* have been using to proceed from Plumstead, beneath the Thames, to North Woolwich. (DarkestElephant via Wikimedia Commons CC SA 3.0)

by rotating arms which are behind the cutting head. Seven segments weighing 3,000kg and a keystone weighing 1,000kg form one ring, which lines approximately 1.5m of excavated tunnel. The segments vary in shape to accommodate the curves in the line as the TBM moves forward and once they are in place concrete grout is sprayed through apertures to seal them into place in the surrounding clay or chalk beneath London. The tunnel face is monitored by pressure sensors and a laser guidance system ensures that the machine moves in the correct direction, with a tolerance of about 1mm.

The machines were made to two separate designs. *Sophia* and *Mary*, which drove the tunnels beneath the Thames between North Woolwich and Plumstead, were smaller slurry machines, designed to deal with the chalk, sand and gravel beneath the river, while the remaining machines were earth pressure balance machines, which are better suited to the London clay and gravel through which they had to bore. The distance bored by each machine and the timings were as follows:

Phyllis	Royal Oak to Farringdon	6.8 km	May 2012– Oct 2013
Ada		6.8km	August 2012– Jan 2014
Elizabeth	Limmo Peninsula, Canning Town, to Farringdon	8.3 km	Nov 2012– May 2015
Victoria		8.3km	Dec 2012– June 2015
Jessica	Pudding Mill Lane to Stepney Green	2.7 km	Aug 2013– Feb 2014
Ellie		2.7km	Feb 2014– June 2014
Jessica	Limmo Peninsula, Canning Town to Victoria Dock	0.9km	June 2014– Aug 2014
Ellie		0.9km	Sept 2014– Oct 2014
Sophia	Plumstead to North Woolwich	2.9km	Jan 2013– Jan 2014
Mary		2.9km	May 2013– May 2014

It has been calculated that the TBMs averaged 38m per day over the length of the project with the maximum being achieved by *Ellie* on 16 April 2014 when she excavated 72m between Pudding Mill Lane and Stepney Green. Had *Ellie* been available to Marc Brunel she could have completed the tunnel in less than a week rather than the eighteen years it took. But then she is an Olympic athlete! In the same year that

Ellie created this record, an Artist in Residence was appointed to the project. The work in progress was recorded, featuring the people and activities both at the construction sites themselves and those living near them. A group of children aged 8–15 from Tower Hamlets visited the Liverpool Street site after which they used iPads to create digital artworks based on their experiences of the site during their visit.

THE END OF TUNNELLING

On 4 June 2015, after *Victoria* broke through the last segment of clay to reach Farringdon station, Prime Minister David Cameron and Boris Johnson attended a ceremony to mark the end of tunnelling. The last segment of concrete was slotted into place and the work of laying rails and installing signalling could be completed. The tunnelling machines were dismantled when their work was done and parts will be reused in other TBMs for future projects. However, *Ada* and *Phyllis* were both buried close to where they finished tunnelling at Farringdon as it was not feasible to remove them and one of *Phyllis's* cutting teeth was buried at Farringdon in a time capsule that also contained a copy of the *London A-Z* which sealed her namesake's reputation.

The work of laying the tracks continued for a further two years, the completion of the process being marked by a short ceremony at Whitechapel station on 14 September 2017. Special sleepers have been used in parts of the central area to reduce noise and vibration, with further measures taken between Farringdon and Liverpool Street stations to ensure that plays and concerts at the Barbican Centre are not disturbed by noise from the trains: one of five different types of track laid to accommodate the needs of the terrain through and beneath which the trains run. This contrasts with the opening of the Central Line in 1900 when the noise and vibrations from the trains with their large, powerful American loco-motives gave rise to complaints that draughtsmen were unable to draw straight lines in the offices above the railway. Farringdon is the largest station on Crossrail and the hub of the network with links to the Circle, Metropolitan and Hammersmith & City Lines and to main-line services to Luton and Gatwick airports. It is a particularly large station with tunnel diameters of 25m, twice the size of normal Underground stations, and the platforms are 250m in length (compared with 120m for conventional underground stations) to accommodate the nine-car Crossrail trains.

CONCRETE TUNNEL SEGMENTS

As the TBMs advanced, prefabricated concrete tunnel segments were manoeuvred into place by machinery, a process long used in the construction of the Underground tunnels and much quicker than Marc Brunel's bricklayers. Each segment weighs 3.4 tons and is 30cm thick, and each ring required seven segments and a keystone. A quarter of a million were required in total. Of these, 110,000

Tunnel segments, made at Old Oak Common, stored at Willesden and awaiting collection for insertion in the Crossrail tunnels. Each tunnel ring required seven segments and a smaller keystone, these visible just to the right of the centre of this picture. A quarter of a million were required to complete the tunnels, each of them approximately 30cm thick. (Marcus Rowland via Wikimedia Commons CC SA 3.0)

were manufactured in a specially-built factory at Chatham in Kent, where the Medway valley provides an ample supply of the materials required for the concrete; 75,000 were made at a factory at Old Oak Common, close to the Western entrance to the tunnels at Royal Oak; and a factory at Mulligar in Ireland made the segments used in the Thames tunnel between Plumstead and North Woolwich. River barges were used to move the segments from Chatham to the Limmo Peninsula, Canning Town.

A NEW NATURE RESERVE

More than 7 million tons of material was excavated for Crossrail. About half of it was extracted from tunnels, 20 –42m beneath the surface, and the rest in connection with work sinking shafts and building stations closer to the surface. What was to become of this mass, consisting mostly of chalk, gravel and clay?

At the greater depths (the lowest point being at Finsbury Circus near Liverpool Street station) it is free of pollution, and although it does not contain the nutrients required for growing crops it can provide an underpinning for soil that does. It was first pumped, as slurry, to a processing centre in Plumstead where the water was squeezed out and the residue turned into 'cakes' of spoil: enough to fill Wembley stadium three times. Some of this was used for landfill at Rainham, Pitsea and Ockendon in Essex, and at Calvert, near Bicester. At Fairlop in Redbridge, Greater London, it was used for agricultural land, and in the Ingrebourne Valley at Havering, Greater London, it has gone to a golf course. At Kingsnorth on the Isle of Grain in the Medway Estuary it will underpin an industrial park.

However, about half the total has been devoted to creating two nature reserves, one at East Tilbury in Essex and the other, much larger and more ambitious, at Wallasea Island. The island lies close to the mouth of Essex's River Crouch where it meets the mouth of the River Roach before entering the North Sea. In December 2011 the civil engineering company BAM Nuttall Ltd and a Dutch company called

Van Oord, which specialises in drainage and land reclamation, were awarded a contract to transport the material by barges to Wallasea.

Little is known about the history of this obscure corner of Essex. It may have been used as a source of salt extracted from the North Sea in Roman times. During the Middle Ages it was probably part of about 30,000 hectares of tidal salt marshes along the Essex coast, providing homes for fish and sea birds without number. A sea wall was constructed in the fifteenth century, possibly by Dutch settlers, and the island was using for grazing and, more recently, for growing wheat on the silt deposited at the end of the last Ice Age about 10,000 years ago. In the late nineteenth century there were as many as 135 inhabitants, and the island has also been home to a rather windy campsite and a marina with a ferry connection to Burnham-on-Crouch to the north. The island has often been flooded, most notably during the great storm and flood of 1953 when much of East Anglia was inundated, with many lives lost. Following this catastrophe, large sections of the sea wall were rebuilt and wheat is cultivated, but at high tide the island is 2m below sea level and is constantly at risk of catastrophic flooding by salt water, which does nothing for a wheat crop. In 2006 much of the sea wall was bulldozed, beginning the process of creating wetlands for a nature reserve.

Wallasea Island: the sea wall, designed to protect the island from flooding. The wall has now been breached to admit the sea and create a nature reserve of 670 hectares of wetlands, much of it salt marsh, which will be the largest in Europe, underpinned by 3 million tons of spoil from Crossrail and attracting hundreds of thousands of birds. (Peter Slaughter vi Wikimedia Commons)

A yellow wagtail visiting Wallasea Island, one of many species which the RSPB hopes to attract to the new nature reserve built on the Crossrail debris. (Dan Davison via Wikimedia Commons CC 2.0)

Salt marsh on Wallasea Island. Not an attractive prospect for most human visitors but a wonderful habitat for seabirds and those who enjoy observing them. (John Myers via Wikimedia Commons CC 2.0)

In 2008, as the Crossrail Bill reached its final stages, the Royal Society for the Protection of Birds (RSPB) approached Essex County Council with a plan to demolish the remaining sea walls and turn the whole island into a wetland nature reserve, using material excavated by the Crossrail tunnelling to raise its level by 2m and turn the island into a labyrinth of lagoons, streams, mudflats and salt marshes of the kind that Wallasea accommodated before the first sea wall was built, to be called the Wallasea Island Wild Coast Project. At present there are 30,000 sea birds living on 100 hectares of salt marsh off the Essex coast. The new Wallasea Island reserve will increase that almost sevenfold with about 670 hectares of additional wetland, together with footpaths and cycle paths. It is anticipated that this abundance will attract lost breeding populations of spoonbills and Kentish plovers back to the area as well as avocet, dunlin, redshank and lapwings, together with wintering flocks of Brent geese, wigeon and curlew. Saltwater fish like bass, herring and flounder are also expected to colonise the wetlands and provide food for the seal colony which still populates the area.

In September 2102, as *Phyllis* and *Ada* headed for Farringdon, the first delivery of Crossrail spoil arrived at Wallasea to begin the creation of Europe's largest man-made nature reserve. It arrived by water, loaded on to boats near the Limmo Peninsula, Canning Town, and was followed by similar consignments over the following four years until the tunnelling was complete, following which the RSPB arranged for the delivery of earth to overlay the clay and chalk and provide a fertile base for the growing of wild flowers and other crops on the island's surface. This use of the spoil is in some contrast with the practice of the tunnellers' Victorian predecessors. In the nineteenth century, as the Victorians built the Underground railways and the sewers, much of the spoil was taken to Stamford Creek in Fulham, west London, where in 1877 it was used to create embankments from which spectators could watch the activities of the London Athletic Club. By that time the ground was known as Stamford Bridge and in the early twentieth century the ground was acquired by two brothers, Gus and Joseph Mears, who used it as the stadium for the football club they founded: Chelsea.

8

STATIONS, SIGNALS AND TRAINS

The stations served by Crossrail are given below from west to east with branches:

Reading • Twyford • Maidenhead • Taplow • Burnham • Slough • Langley • Iver • West Drayton • Hayes & Harlington (branch line to Heathrow with services to terminals 2–5) • Southall • Hanwell • West Ealing • Ealing Broadway • Acton • Paddington • Bond Street • Tottenham Court Road. • Farringdon • Liverpool Street • Whitechapel

At Stepney, beyond Whitechapel, the line forks. To the south it proceeds to:

Canary Wharf • Custom House • Woolwich • Abbey Wood: the south-eastern terminus

To the east it proceeds to:

Stratford • Maryland • Forest Gate • Manor Park • Ilford • Seven Kings • Goodmayes • Chadwell Heath • Romford • Gidea Park • Harold Wood • Brentwood • Shenfield: the Essex terminus

There were attempts to gain stations for other communities on the route. Silvertown Station, on the North London Line, was closed in 2006 and services were withdrawn; and the nearby London City Airport offered to contribute £50 million to the construction of a station on the Crossrail line, between Custom House and Woolwich, which would be attractive to airport users. The case was not made and the former Silvertown station was in fact demolished in connection with the construction of the Crossrail route. It remains a possibility for the future. The Royal Borough of Kensington and Chelsea also campaigned for a station on the former site of the Kensal Gasworks near Ladbroke Grove, possibly called Portobello station, believing that it would regenerate an ill-favoured area in the north of that wealthy borough which later suffered the tragic Grenfell Tower fire. Boris Johnson was a strong advocate, arguing that it would generate 5,000 new homes and 2,000 jobs, but in 2013 Transport for London reached the view that it was not financially feasible and Sadiq Khan, Boris Johnson's successor, did not share his enthusiasm.

The Crossrail Route as finally
determined after much debate.

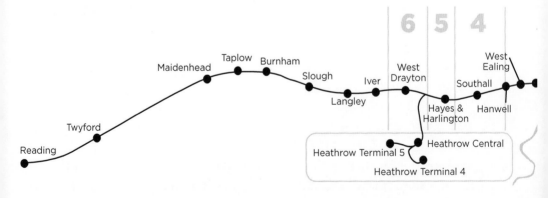

Brunel's Paddington station, now joined by Crossrail's. (Elahuguet via Wikimedia Commons CC SA 1.0)

Portobello Road is home to a famous street market but not, despite its best efforts, to a Crossrail station. (Simonttx via Wikimedia Commons)

Construction of the stations in the central area presented a fresh set of challenges. These were partly caused by the fact that they are all situated in areas densely occupied both by buildings and people. The sheer size of the stations was also a problem. The trains are over 200m in length served by platforms measuring 240m, so long that it was considered necessary to have entrances at each end of most of the stations. Passengers using Tottenham Court Road station would not want to walk from Charing Cross Road to a ticket hall beyond Soho Square to enter the Crossrail station. Moreover, those who use the Underground will be aware that as a train enters a station it pushes air before it, creating a strong, warm and rarely comfortable draught of air. And as it leaves the station it creates a partial vacuum as there is a withdrawal of air. With trains of 200m in length (Northern and Piccadilly Line trains are 108m long) and a larger tunnel (6.2m compared with 3.5m) the draught would be stressful so it was necessary to create larger station spaces to absorb the heat and energy.

AUSTRIAN TUNNELLING

This was achieved in part by using the New Austrian Tunnelling Method (NATM), which was devised in Austria in the early 1960s as a means of tunnelling beneath the Alps. It makes optimum use of the inherent strength of the rock through which the tunnel is being bored, carefully monitoring its behaviour as tunnelling proceeds and using sprayed concrete to seal in place a load-bearing structure. The running tunnels of Crossrail are of uniform shape and size and suitable for the installation of concrete segments, but the NATM is particularly useful in creating the larger, irregularly shaped spaces required for the very large stations which Crossrail needs to accommodate its exceptionally long trains. The method also makes it possible to create smoother curves for the stations, which are aesthetically more pleasing and less prone to sudden draughts of air. Voids with extractor fans beneath the platforms have also been created to absorb some of the heat and impact of the moving air mass.

NEW STATIONS AND A NEW MAP

Ten of the stations, while bearing the names for stations that already exist on the network, are of such a scale that they may be described as virtually new creations. In order to prepare the designs for these new stations, a dummy station was constructed in a well-concealed location, 40 miles north of London, at the Vinci technology centre in Leighton Buzzard, Bedfordshire. It had two platforms, connected by a passageway, with station furniture such as seats, lights, signs and public address systems as well as escalators and lifts. It used a variety of materials to test their suitability for the new stations with their unusual dimensions.

One of the aims of the design team was to reduce station clutter, and in this they were following the precepts laid down in the 1930s by the stern figure of Frank Pick, vice chairman and chief executive of the London Transport network during the 1930s.

A blue plaque on Frank Pick's former home at 15 Wildwood Road, Hampstead Garden Suburb. He was a pioneer of good design on London Transport. (Spudgun67 via Wikimedia Commons CC SA 4.0)

A blue plaque marking the Leyton birthplace of Harry Beck, electrical draughtsman and designer of the iconic Underground Map. (Spudgun67 via Wikimedia Commons CC SA 4.0)

Frank Pick (1878-1941) was one of the most influential figures in the history of the Underground, and particularly in connection with its art and architecture. Born in Lincolnshire, he moved to the Underground in 1906 and was a founder member of the Design and Industries Association which advocated modern design incorporating new materials and methods. In 1932, after some hesitation, he adopted the new design for the Underground map proposed by a temporarily unemployed electrical draughtsman, Harry Beck (1902–74). It became an icon of industrial design and, updated to accommodate new lines, remains in use.

In the 1930s, Pick commissioned the architect Charles Holden (1875–1960) to design new stations on the Northern Line extension between Clapham and Morden. Pick informed one correspondent, 'We are going to discard entirely all ornament ... We are going to represent the Design and Industries Association gone mad.' Holden later designed stations on the northern extension of the Piccadilly Line, many of them now listed buildings.

Pick hated clutter. When, in 1931, he visited Sudbury Town station following its redesign by Holden, he was appalled by what he saw as the muddle on the platforms. He wrote a furious letter, in withering terms, to the unfortunate engineer responsible:

> Automatic machines have been dumped down and are now going to spoil the cleanness and clearness of the platforms ... there seems to be a desire on the part of everyone to break up and destroy the tidiness of this station ... I wish you to take no action to remedy the defects to which I have drawn attention. I wish Sudbury Town station to remain exactly as it is as a permanent memorial to the department that cannot do its work properly.

Pick also commissioned early works from many artists who later became famous in the form of posters to promote Underground travel. These included the writer and artist Len Deighton, McKnight Kauffer, Frank Brangwyn and Mabel Lucie Attwell. And Pick's legacy has continued in other forms, notably in projects such as the Poems on the Underground, launched in the 1980s, and Maths on the Underground, launched in 2000.

DAYLIGHT AND SEDUM

Several features of the new stations would surely have earned the approval of Frank Pick. Even in the stations well beneath the surface efforts have been made to admit natural light and the roofs of one station, as described below, will be covered with sedum plants which absorb carbon dioxide, require virtually no care and can survive long periods of drought with their thick, moisture-storing leaves.

Those who use the Underground will be familiar with the deafening level of announcements whose volume is exceeded only by their inaudibility. Thought has been given to improving the acoustic qualities of the stations. It is anticipated that the larger spaces and gentler

A sedum plant, a species used on the roof of Whitechapel station. A very resilient plant, it requires little care, absorbs carbon dioxide and can survive severe drought. (Semolo75 via Wikimedia Commons)

curves of the new stations, achieved by sprayed concrete surfaces and sound absorbent panels in light fittings, will enable quieter, clearer messages to be more effectively delivered, aided by loudspeakers in the station signs, known as finger posts or totems which direct passengers to exits and connecting services.

Within the stations, platform screens, similar to those used on the Jubilee Line, will further reduce noise and draughts, as well as improving safety, and above the screens themselves will be bands with information about approaching trains, punctuality and conditions elsewhere on the network.

Materials and decorative features of the stations have been selected to reflect the areas in which they are situated: for example the entertainment quarter in Soho, to the west of Tottenham Court Road station; the grand thoroughfares which surround Bond Street station; the Hatton Garden jewellers, the light engineering traditions and the creative industries which surround Farringdon; and the ultra-modern citadels of Canary Wharf.

Opportunities have also been taken to design spacious station approaches and pedestrian-friendly forecourts and to develop residential, retail and office space where the redevelopment associated with the stations has released suitable land. It is estimated that twelve substantial buildings and a total of about 3 million sq.ft of new space has been created in this way, some of the proceeds of the development contributing to the cost of the Crossrail project. Such is the size of the new stations, extending over a little less than a kilometre, that ticket halls at either end of the stations often reflect the differing ambiences of the areas in which they are situated.

The Crossrail Art Foundation has been created as a registered charity with support from the City of London Corporation to commission public art for seven of the Crossrail stations in the central area: Paddington; Bond Street; Tottenham Court Road; Farringdon; Liverpool Street; Whitechapel and Canary Wharf. Seven art galleries, based in London, will work with Crossrail to enhance these stations in what will amount to a public art gallery.

The new stations are built according to three models:

Mined stations are created initially by tunnelling and then carved out into the size required and secured with sprayed concrete.

Boxed stations are created by building concrete retaining walls just beneath the surface, which serve as a framework within which the station is built.

Above-ground stations are built outside the central area.

The distinctive design features of the stations in the central area are as follows, running eastwards from Paddington, and the station designs have been sponsored by the City of London Corporation, together with such bodies as Heathrow Airport, Goldman Sachs and Canary Wharf Group:

Paddington

The original station was designed and built by Isambard Kingdom Brunel with the architect Matthew Digby Wyatt. As so often, the workaholic Victorian engineer was in a hurry, writing to Wyatt in 1851, 'I am going to design, in a great hurry, a station after my own fancy,' and informing Wyatt that he would welcome his advice and assistance. Brunel's station, now a Grade I listed building, was opened in 1854. It is hard to imagine such a project being completed in so short a time in the twenty-first century.

The new station has had to be located in an area busy with pedestrian and vehicle traffic and give easy access to main-line trains, four Underground services (District, Circle, Bakerloo and Hammersmith & City) and the new Crossrail services to Reading, Heathrow and central London. It has also had to complement, and even compete with, Brunel's magnificent structure. The new station is built immediately to the south of Brunel's, where the taxi rank once was. Its construction was facilitated by alterations to Brunel's station involving the construction of a new concourse close to the Grand Union Canal and the new taxi rank. The Crossrail station is on three levels, with the first, at ground level, surmounted by a glazed roof with a stone pavement lined by shops and restaurants adjacent to the main-line platforms. The roof is covered throughout its length with a canopy on which is printed a design by the American artist Spencer Finch, which depicts the sky in such a way that it will seem to change with the time of day and the position of the sun. There will also be an area devoted to shops and cafes from which passengers can walk across to the main-line station or pass down to Crossrail services. Beneath this is the ticket hall and concourse and 20m below the surface are the platforms where the lighting, set in concrete ceiling recesses, are of a circular lily pad design.

Bond Street

Mined, 28m below the surface, Bond Street station stretches from Hanover Square westwards to Davies Street, with a ticket hall at each end. Bond Street exists only as the name of this station and on the Monopoly Board as the local station for the grandest of all its locations, Mayfair, though New Bond Street and Old Bond Street do exist and pass above the new station. Colonnades mark the entrances to both ticket halls, though at the Hanover Square ticket hall the design, in pale Portland Stone, reflects the architectural grandeur of the square itself with the magnificent colonnaded entrance of the eighteenth-century St George's Hanover Square, the parish church of Mayfair nearby. The entrance to the Davies Street ticket hall is in the more homely red sandstone and bronze, reflecting the more domestic character of the equally exclusive London Street. Over the Hanover Square entrance an eight-storey building is being constructed of retail, office and residential space. Following the opening of the new Crossrail service a number of bus services along Oxford Street will be withdrawn. Moreover the availability of entrances and ticket offices at each end of Bond Street and Tottenham Court Road stations will, it is hoped, make it possible for the street to be pedestrianised between Oxford Circus and Orchard Street, east of Marble Arch, a long-sought aim of London mayors which is planned to coincide with the launch of Elizabeth Line services.

Tottenham Court Road

Tottenham Court Road station has long been noted for the artworks of Eduardo Paolozzi which were installed in the 1980s and reflect the entertainment traditions of the area. To these have now been added colourful geometric designs of the French artist Daniel Buren. The new station, mined, and 24m below ground level, stretches almost a kilometre from Charing Cross Road beneath Soho Square to Dean Street in the heart of Soho. The eastern ticket hall is six times the size of that of the old station, with white glass to admit light and stainless steel to reflect the modern architecture of the thirty-three-storey Centre Point, built in the 1960s, which is a short distance

A large hole in the ground in 2010 on the edge of Soho is early evidence of plans for the new Crossrail station which will soon begin to emerge. (Mark Kobayashi-Hillary via Wikimedia Commons CC 2.0)

A Crossrail casualty: the popular Bath House pub in Soho was demolished to make way for the new station. (Ewan Munro, via Wikimedia Commons CC 2.0)

from the eastern entrance across a pedestrian plaza that has been constructed at St Giles Circus. The ceiling is decorated with a gold leaf pattern. In contrast to the light-filled entrance at the St Giles end of the station, the Dean Street entrance has black glass to reflect the nightlife associated with Soho and the former Bath House pub which once stood in the area.

Farringdon

Mined, 30m below ground, this station, where Crossrail meets Thameslink and the Tube, Farringdon will be one of the busiest in the entire rail network with 140 trains passing through it daily – appropriately, since this was the original terminus for the Metropolitan Railway in 1863. The station will be a hub that will enable passengers to make such journeys as Cambridge to Heathrow or Reading to Brighton with only one change. The new station stretches from Long Lane, near Smithfield Market, to Cowcross Street and the designs, supported by Goldman Sachs and the City of London Corporation, are the work of the British artist Simon Periton. The eastern ticket hall, in Long Lane, admits natural light through triangular structures on the roof and its internal architecture will reflect the concrete 'brutalist' style of the nearby Barbican, while the external glazing reflects the intricate Victorian ironwork of Sir Horace Jones's design for nearby Smithfield Market. In the western ticket hall, diamond-shaped patterns are a feature of the ceilings above the escalators and the diamond theme is also echoed on the interior walls, a reference to the fact that the entrance is in the vicinity of Hatton Garden. For reasons that remain a mystery, the Thameslink services are currently absent from the iconic London Underground map. Perhaps this is the time to include them.

Liverpool Street

Mined, 34m beneath the surface, this is the deepest of the new stations. It extends from Old Broad Street beneath Finsbury Circus, London's oldest public park dating to 1606, to Moorgate. Here the site was exceptionally constrained by the fact that the area was already extensively occupied by large, modern buildings and the two ticket halls,

Destruction precedes construction at the site of the Farringdon Crossrail station in 2011 in this busy corner on the fringe of the City. (Robin Webster via Wikimedia Commons CC SA 2.0)

No. 43 Hatton Garden, formerly a church, then a home known as Wren House, now available as office space in a listed building designed by Christopher Wren in Hatton Garden close to the western entrance to Farringdon station. (Elisa.rolle via Wikimedia Commons CC SA 4.0)

The sign marking the Clerks' Well commemorates the original name of the area, Clerkenwell, in the midst of which the Farringdon Crossrail station is situated. It was a precious source of water before tap water became available. (Spudgun67 via Wikimedia Commons Cc SA 4.0)

at each end of the station, each connect to a different underground station: Liverpool Street to the east and Moorgate to the west. The long, thin lines of the ceiling panels reflect the pin stripes of many of the City financiers who will pass beneath them.

Whitechapel

Mined, 30m beneath the surface, one of its entrances is that of the old Whitechapel Underground station; the other, to the north, is on Durward Street. The two are linked by a station roof that is unique on the London Transport network, being planted with Sedum. This plant absorbs carbon, acts as an effective insulator and requires minimal attention. Even during prolonged droughts it can draw on the water it stores in its thick leaves. The escalator hall at the northern end of the station will feature the notation of the change ring known as *Whitechapel Round Surprise Major*, to reflect that the famous Whitechapel Bell Foundry was casting bells at its premises on the opposite side of Whitechapel road for over 400 years from 1570 until it relocated in 2017. The original site is listed and preserved.

Canary Wharf

A boxed design, the length of this building is the same as the Shard is high, 310m, and considerably longer than the height of the adjacent No. 1 Canada Square. It emerges from the dock that surrounds it, like a tea clipper, with the platforms themselves 28m beneath the dock, which had to be drained of 98 million litres of water before the station could be built. Above the platforms are five levels of station facilities and retail space, together with a cinema, surmounted by a roof

The entrance to Whitechapel station on Whitechapel Road remains a feature of the much extended Crossrail station. Beyond Whitechapel the Crossrail lines fork, with one service running east to Shenfield, Essex and the other passing beneath the river to Abbey Wood and Kent. (bob walker via Wikimedia Commons CC SA 2.0)

The Crossrail station at Canary Wharf emerges from the water like a ship about to set sail: five levels topped with its glulam roof, which admits light and rainwater to the unusual plants within the conservatory. (The wub via Wikimedia Commons CC SA 4.0)

garden within a conservatory containing plants of the kind formerly imported to the wharf from the West Indies and the Canary Islands – the latter gave their name to the dock in its heyday. The conservatory roof is of novel design, from Austria: a lattice of glulam (1,500 glued, laminated timber beams) prefabricated in Austria and assembled on site. Once installed, air-filled 'pillows' were inserted into the lattice structure. The method echoed that adopted by Joseph Paxton for the Crystal Palace as described in chapter 1. They require little maintenance and admit both rainwater and sunlight to the conservatory. The station itself features images by the artist Michael Rovner depicting the movement of people through the station.

Custom House

This above-ground station was built on a very constricted site: a long, thin space between the Dockland Light Railway and Victoria Dock Road. The components were made in a factory in Nottinghamshire and taken by road 150 miles to be installed on site between the ExCel exhibition centre and the residential areas of the Borough of Newham to the north. A steel frame contains air-filled pillows similar to those used at Canary Wharf and at the Eden Project in Cornwall.

Woolwich

Woolwich station, a late addition to the Crossrail scheme, is a boxed design, 14m below the surface as the railway prepares to descend beneath the Thames towards North Woolwich. It is close to the site of the former Royal Arsenal (the original home of Arsenal football club) where artillery and explosives were made and tested and medals were cast in bronze. It finally closed in the 1990s. The station's design reflects this rich history. The entrance is framed in bronze decorated in a pattern that reflects the rifling within the barrel of an artillery piece known as the Woolwich System. It will also feature a Dead Man's Penny, a bronze memorial plaque presented to the next of kin of servicemen killed in the First World War, engraved with an image of Britannia, a lion and the words 'He died for freedom and honour' together with the name of the deceased. The plaques were made at the Royal Arsenal from 1920.

Woolwich Arsenal: formerly the home of an ordnance works, a military academy which produced General Gordon and a rather well-known football club before they moved to Highbury and later to the Emirates Stadium. Now, after much negotiation, it has a station on the Crossrail service. (Fin Fahey via Wikimedia Commons CC SA 2.5)

Abbey Wood

Above ground, this is a major transformation of the former small Abbey Wood station. It has the longest platforms on the system at 260m and opened on 22 October 2017. The spectacular roof of the new station resembles a stingray. The boundary between the London Boroughs of Bexley and Greenwich runs through the station and Bexley is one of the few London Boroughs that has neither Tube nor Docklands Light Railway service and anticipates a major boost to the local economy from Crossrail. It is working with the neighbouring Greenwich Council and the Peabody Trust (which provides social housing) to deliver thousands of new homes to be delivered following the opening of Crossrail services.

SIGNALLING

Within the central area the trains will be run under Automatic Train Operation similar to that introduced on the Victoria Line in 1967, each train being operated by one person, instead of a driver and a guard. The operator, in the driver's cab, opens and closes the doors and operates the 'start' mechanism when the train is ready to leave the station. Trackside sensors feed information to computers, which activate a display within the driver's cab, giving information on the condition of the line ahead. The system adjusts the speed of the train to optimise tunnel usage as well as stopping it at stations. Trains are also equipped with a communication system so that, in an emergency, the operator can contact the control centre. The Victoria Line was the first in the world to adopt such a system on the initiative of the Underground's Chief Signal Engineer, Robert Dell. The Jubilee Line, which entered service in 1979, operates in the same way. Eight years later, in 1987, the Docklands Light Railway took the system a step further, dispensing with a driver in the cabin though retaining one operator on board to check the opening and closing of doors. These systems, however, are self-contained and do not interact with the traditional Absolute Block system which operates on main-line railways.

The Absolute Block system, first introduced in Great Britain in the mid-nineteenth century and made compulsory in 1889, divides the track into sections, entry to each section being controlled by a signal. Each section can contain only one train at a time and a following train can only enter it when the signalman (or computer) registers that the train has moved into the section ahead, at which point the signal is changed from 'stop' to 'proceed'. In the years that followed its introduction the semaphore signals indicating 'stop' and 'proceed' were replaced by coloured lights which reflected the distance before the train ahead: red (stop, train immediately ahead); yellow (proceed with caution, train two sections ahead); double yellow (train three sections ahead); and green (track ahead clear). The drivers of the Crossrail trains, when they emerge from the automatic control of the central area, will have to cope with these conditions and the system will also have to take account of the fact that, at some junctions, Crossrail interacts with trains from other lines which are not under automatic control. There are long-term plans for replacing the Absolute Block system with one which informs the driver in his cab of the state of the line ahead, but that is so far ahead that it won't help Crossrail. When questioned about possible difficulties arising from these interfaces the Crossrail project chairman said that a 'mitigation plan' would be implemented if required. The whole system will be managed from the Elizabeth Line Control Centre at Romford, which was completed towards the end of 2017.

THE TRAINS

The contract for the manufacture of the trains was awarded in 2014 to Bombardier Transportation, to be built at their works in Derby. The design, known as Aventra 345, is based upon rolling stock which has been used on Thameslink services. Approximately seventy-three trainsets will enter service, with a maintenance depot at Old Oak Common, the value of the contract being altogether approximately £1 billion. The trains are designed to accommodate 450 seated passengers and about 1,000 standing (bearing in mind that many journeys in the busy central area will be short ones between Underground stations), with a speed of up to 90mph. A seven-carriage unit entered service between Liverpool Street and Shenfield on 22 June 2017, though it is anticipated that when platforms have been lengthened to 240m the trains will increase in size to nine-car units. They will be operated entirely by the driver, who will receive in his cab pictures from the platform generated by CCTV. The trains will all be 'walk-through' like the newer Underground trains, with free Wi-Fi in all carriages. In October 2017 the new trains passed through part of the central Crossrail tunnels for the first time, with supply trains passing routinely from the portals at Plumstead and Pudding Mill Lane to the Royal Oak portal from that time.

New Crossrail rolling stock about to set off from the Essex Crossrail terminus at Shenfield to Liverpool Street station in July 2017. Regular services using the new stock began a few weeks earlier. (Sunil060902 via Wikimedia Commons CC SA 4.0)

9

HEROIC ENGINEERING

THE EYE OF THE NEEDLE

Creating a tunnel 26 miles in length with a diameter of 6.2 metres beneath central London presents challenges different from those posed even by the Channel Tunnel or those through mountain ranges like the Alps. Apart from the sheer scale of the operation, there was the need to thread the new structure though the web of tunnels already existing, some created by nature and others by human activity. For example, there is a network of rivers beneath the city which are older than London itself: the Fleet, the Westbourne, the Wandle, the Walbrook and the Tyburn to name but a few. They are for the most part concealed beneath the streets but still conduct rainwater to the Thames. The best known, and most visible, is the Fleet which, besides giving its name to Fleet Street and the old Fleet Prison for debtors, is a substantial river flowing from Hampstead Heath beneath Farringdon Road into the Thames just upstream from Blackfriars station. Its outlet into the Thames may be glimpsed from the station platforms at low tide. These streams presented major obstacles to engineers who, from the Middle Ages onwards, created street sewers though in many cases the sewers diverted rainwater and waste water from buildings into the rivers themselves.

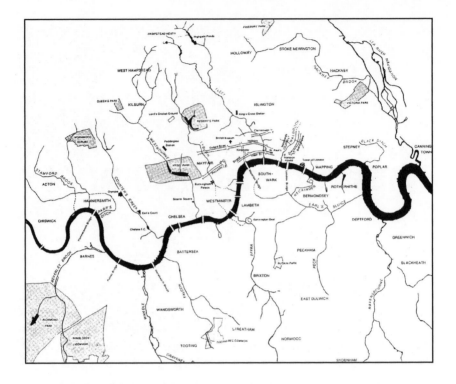

London's underground rivers: apart from the Thames itself, London has an extensive network of rivers flowing beneath the capital, as can be seen from this map. (Courtesy of Thames Water plc)

DRAINS AND TRAINS

From the early nineteenth century onwards the increasing flow of waste water into the rivers led to the pollution of the Thames which, in turn, led to the construction of a new system of intercepting sewers by Sir Joseph Bazalgette in the Victorian period (see chapter 1). He constructed 82 miles of large intercepting sewers, running from west to east across the capital, north and south of the Thames, to collect waste water including sewage from streets and buildings and conduct it to treatment works at Barking, on the north bank of the Thames and Crossness, near Abbey Wood on the south bank, Abbey Wood also being of course the south-eastern terminus of Crossrail. The intercepting sewers have a diameter varying from less than 2m, at their western end, to more than 6m as they approach the treatment works in the east. In addition, Bazalgette added 1,100 miles of street sewers and in the process he had to weave his network through the existing complex of rivers, canals and railways. Late in life Bazalgette, in an interview for a magazine, explained the problems. He told the interviewer:

> I get most credit for the Thames Embankment, but it wasn't anything like such a job as the drainage … the fall in the river isn't above three inches a mile; for sewage we want a couple of feet and that kept taking us down below the river and when we got to a certain depth we had to pump up again. It was certainly a very troublesome job. We would sometimes spend weeks drawing our plans and then suddenly come across some railway or canal that upset everything and we had to begin all over again. It was tremendously hard work. I was living over at Morden then, and often used to drive down there from my office at twelve or one o'clock in the morning.

Bazalgette began his great drainage work in the 1850s and completed it in the 1870s, by which time other underground obstacles had been created. The Metropolitan Line had been opened in 1863 and was followed by others, amounting to 113 miles of large-diameter tunnels beneath the surface. And of course there are the many thousands of miles of pipework for water supplies, gas and electricity – not all of them as accurately mapped as later engineers might wish. And also we must remember the existing network of Underground railways in the central area. It was through this complex web that Crossrail had to find its way and the new tunnel, of course, is not in the suburbs but passes through the area with the densest network of all. It also passes beneath many of London's most historic structures. In the circumstances some of the engineering challenges were of the highest order.

THE STOCKLEY FLYOVER

In fact the first major engineering work was not a tunnel at all but a flyover at Stockley, just to the west of Hayes and Harlington station, completed in November 2014. A new bridge was built to enable Crossrail trains to reach Heathrow airport without the need for them to cross the Great Western main line which at this point has four tracks. Given the frequency of Crossrail trains to Heathrow this would have caused intolerable delays to the busy main line so a new flyover was built by Carillion to enable Crossrail (and in the meantime Heathrow Connect) services to pass over it. The new track is borne up to the flyover on concrete spans and piers and the flyover itself is 120m long, made of weathered steel which is treated so that it will develop an oxide layer to protect the metal from further rusting so that it will never need painting. What a pity they didn't know about that when the Forth Bridge was built. The new flyover is already in use, the longest single-span bridge on the Great Western Railway since the days of Brunel.

THE EYE OF THE NEEDLE

In the summer of 2014 the BBC broadcast a documentary called The *Fifteen Billion Pound Railway* about the construction of Crossrail. One of the highlights of the series of three programmes (and certainly the most tense for one viewer) features the process that the contractors called 'the eye of the needle'. This followed the progress as TBM *Phyllis*, by now a very experienced tunneller, made her way through a particularly complex web of tunnels beneath Tottenham Court Road Underground station. Those who use the station regularly will be aware of the maze of escalators and long underground walkways which connect the Central Line platforms with those of the Northern Line and the station exits. The Crossrail engineers had to place its tunnels through a narrow gap between a pair of escalators 12in above the new tunnel and the Northern Line platforms 36in below and at a time when

Wonderful mosaics at Tottenham Court Road Underground station which, happily, did not descend upon TBM *Phyllis* as she tunnelled through 'the eye of the needle'. (Oxyman via Wikimedia Commons CC 2.5)

the escalators were being used by passengers and trains were running through the platforms. As the TBM cut through the narrow strip of clay between the escalators and the Northern Line, the movement of existing underground structures was monitored by theodolites to ensure that they remained stable until the last concrete segment had been fastened into place. During the whole delicate operation the engineers displayed no signs of concern that the new tunnel would collapse on to the Northern Line or see the escalators above deposit themselves on to the new tunnel. But it is hard to believe that none of them felt any anxiety at the thought that 1,000 tons of TBM was passing 36in above the Northern Line platforms. Similar measures were used to monitor ground movements in other sensitive areas, including The House of St Barnabas, a listed building consisting of a church and charity for the homeless in Soho Square, beneath which the Crossrail Tottenham Court Road station runs. The engineers were no doubt reassured by the fact that they were able to make use, at Tottenham Court Road and elsewhere, of techniques which were applied in the 1990s to measure the disturbance to a much more iconic structure than the platforms of the Northern Line: Big Ben.

COMPENSATION GROUTING: KEEPING BIG BEN UPRIGHT

In the 1990s the Jubilee Line was being constructed beneath Westminster and a new Westminster Underground station was being built beneath Portcullis House. The line, the deepest yet below London, would pass within 34m of the Parliamentary Clock, commonly referred to as Big Ben though that it actually the name of the largest bell, the building itself being named The Elizabeth Tower. Completed in 1858, the world's most famous clock is built on a concrete raft underlaid by gravels and London clay, and when the New Palace Yard car park was built, 16m from the clock and 18m below ground, the clock was found to tilt towards the car park. The excavations for the Jubilee Line are 39m deep and the deeper the tunnel the wider is the expanse of ground disturbed. A tilt beyond about 15mm could cause the clock tower to separate from the adjoining structure of the Palace of Westminster, with untold consequences. To monitor and control the settlement of the clock, 50m-long horizontal steel tubes were installed in the ground beneath the clock where the gravels meet the underlying London clay. Electronic plumb lines were installed to measure the tilt as the tunnelling progressed, and when the tilt reached 15mm, grout (a mixture of cement, sand and water) was ejected through holes in the relevant pipes to compensate for the tilt and bring the tower back to the correct position. Between December 1995 and September 1997 this process continued until the tunnelling had passed the point of disturbance to the structure. Without these measures it is estimated that the tilt would have reached at least 120mm and the clock would have parted company with the rest of the palace.

The clock tower itself is still firmly attached to the adjacent Palace of Westminster. (Adrian Pingstone via Wikimedia Commons)

Big Ben in an engraving of 1858, shortly after the bell was installed in the tower of the clock. The tower is now the Elizabeth Tower and takes its name from HM the Queen; Big Ben is actually the name of the bell. Bell and tower remain in place thanks to compensation grouting, a technique much used on Crossrail to avoid the destabilisation of buildings. (*The Illustrated News of the World*)

The House of St Barnabas, Soho Square, was also saved by the technique of compensation grouting when the Tottenham Court Road Crossrail station passed below Soho Square. (AliceMESewell via Wikimedia Commons CC SA 4.0)

The technique of compensation grouting was also used at Bond Street, Farringdon, Liverpool Street and Whitechapel stations, with twenty-two shafts being sunk at key points from which grouting tubes emerged ready for use when required. But the question may be asked why did Crossrail not avoid these hazardous operations by going deeper than all the existing tunnels and thereby avoid the possibility of disaster? The reasons are threefold. First, the deeper the tunnels run the wider horizontal space their excavation affects, increasing the number of properties that are rendered vulnerable to the tunnelling and therefore needing monitoring, rebalancing and, in case of miscalculation, compensation. Secondly, deeper tunnels would have required more or longer passages and escalators to connect with other underground and main-line railways, lengthening passenger journey times. Bear in mind that every Crossrail station in the central, tunnelled area has more than one connection to existing lines, with Liverpool Street having as many as six. And thirdly, of course, deeper tunnels and longer escalators cost more to build and pose problems of safety in the event of evacuation being required. The choice made was thus a fine balance between cost, time and risk. And since Big Ben and the Northern Line platforms at Tottenham Court Road survived we must assume that the right choices were made.

ELIZABETH: FROM THE OLYMPIC STADIUM TO THE LIMMO PENINSULA BY CRANE

The many who watched the opening ceremony of the London Olympics on 27 July 2012 will no doubt recall the episode in which HM Queen Elizabeth II, accompanied by James Bond, was apparently taken by helicopter to east London and parachuted into the Olympic Stadium. Some believed the evidence of their eyes when the Queen walked into the stadium, apparently unruffled by her adventure. Others were more sceptical and recognised the activities of a stunt double.

A few months later, on 25 October, the TBM bearing the Queen's name was lowered in sections by crane into a 40m-deep shaft on the Limmo Peninsula near Canning Town and reassembled to begin tunnelling towards her destination at Farringdon, 8.3km distant. One of the world's largest cranes was used to lower the TBMs into the shaft, an operation that could only be carried out when there was virtually no wind since, if the giant TBM were to sway into the wall of the shaft itself the damage would be severe for both TBM and the shaft. Soon afterwards *Elizabeth* was joined by *Victoria*, and both TBMs, over the next two years and seven months, made their way to Farringdon where they were greeted by David Cameron and Boris Johnson on 4 June 2015 to mark the conclusion of tunnelling. When the TBMs reached Canary Wharf station they were stopped and given some necessary maintenance before proceeding since the 8.3km of the drive was the greatest undertaken by any of the TBMs. This was the tenth tunnel beneath the Thames excavated by one of the tunnel engineers who began his career in 1964 with the Victoria Line and marked his retirement after fifty years, leaving his two sons to continue the family tunnelling tradition.

LIFT THE POWER STATION AND DON'T INTERRUPT THE VIOLINS

As *Sophia* and *Mary* set out from Plumstead towards the Thames and their destination at North Woolwich, on the northern bank of the river, they first had to negotiate a tunnel beneath an electricity substation at Plumstead that provides power to the North Kent Line of the South-Eastern Railway, which links the Isle of Thanet and the Medway towns to Charing Cross. Engineers pumped in a cushion of sand and gravel to lift the substation by 3cm in order to allow tunnelling to take place without disturbing it.

Similarly, when tunnelling beneath the Barbican to Farringdon, special measures were taken to ensure that the continuous tunnelling of Victoria would not interrupt the performances of the London

Symphony Orchestra in the Barbican Concert Hall. Tunnelling proceeded more slowly at that point and extra measures were taken to insulate the tunnels to ensure that no disturbance occurred.

THE CONNAUGHT TUNNEL

The Eastern Counties & Thames Junction Railway entered service in 1846 to connect east London's Royal Docks, the largest enclosed docks in the world, to the eastern railway network, eventually becoming part of the Great Eastern Railway. In 1878 the railway built two 600ft-long tunnels, running beneath the docks, to connect the new Albert Dock and the North Woolwich ferries to the network. It was in the area known as Silvertown and known as the Connaught Tunnel and also as the Silvertown Tunnel. The roof was in places so close to the bottom of the dock that heavier ships would scrape the roof of the tunnel. The line remained in use until 2006 when the opening of the Docklands Light Railway, together with the opening of the

An engineers' train approaches the Connaught Tunnel during construction work for Crossrail, to expand and clean the ageing Victorian structure. (Kleon3 via Wikimedia Commons CC SA 4.0)

Jubilee Line, left it with little traffic. It was decided to incorporate the disused tunnels into Crossrail for which they had to be cleaned of the grime of 135 years of steam operation and converted to one wider and deeper tunnel to accommodate the Crossrail trains and overhead electrical supply. First, a concrete base was installed on the floor of the dock, with the help of divers, to protect the tunnel. Then the section of the dock above the tunnel had to be sealed off and drained of 13 million litres of river water while the necessary work was completed on the tunnel, though not before fish in the dock had been caught and released to the river. The engineers had six months to complete the work before the dock was refilled to enable Royal Navy vessels to pass to an event at the Exhibition Centre London (ExCel). It was achieved with hours to spare, an event which was one of the highlights of the documentary screened by the BBC on *The Fifteen Billion Pound Railway*.

CASUALTIES: LGBT PARTIES AND MARMALADE JARS

Some structures did not survive the Crossrail tunnellers. Tottenham Court Road Underground station had been built in the nineteenth century to serve the Central Line and, later, the Charing Cross, Euston & Hampstead Railway (later incorporated into the Northern Line). It was built as virtually two separate stations to serve the two lines and, despite later adaptation, was dependent upon long underground corridors to connect the two lines. By the 1960s it was struggling to cope with the volume of passengers travelling to and from the West End, the ticket hall in particular being too cramped for comfort or convenience. By the early years of the twenty-first century 100,000 passengers a day were using the station to embark, disembark or change trains and the number was expected to increase possibly threefold when Crossrail began to call at the station. A major reconstruction of the station was undertaken, with a larger ticket hall and better connections by escalator between the Crossrail, Central and

The Astoria – a cinema, ballroom, nightclub and party venue, and a casualty of the new Crossrail station at Tottenham Court Road. (Ewan Munro from London via Wikimedia Commons CC SA 2.0)

Northern Line platforms. It was also necessary to relocate utilities for electricity, gas and drainage and some casualties were inevitable. The most notable was the London Astoria. It opened in 1927 as a cinema at the northern end of Charing Cross Road, close to its junction with Oxford Street. It occupied the site of a former factory and warehouse which had belonged to the food manufacturer Crosse & Blackwell who occupied premises between Soho Square and Charing Cross Road from 1838 to 1921, manufacturing jams, pickles and other preserves. Crosse & Blackwell moved to Branston in Staffordshire in 1921. The Astoria subsequently became a ballroom, theatre, nightclub and live music venue and was associated with London's LGBT scene, hosting New Year parties. It was closed and demolished in 2009, despite some public opposition, along with a dozen other Soho properties. It is possible that when Crossrail works are completed its site will once again become available for redevelopment. In the meantime a home is sought for the 13,000 nineteenth- and twentieth-century pickle and jam jars which were recovered from the site when excavating the former premises of Crosse & Blackwell. They also recovered some Keiller Marmalade jars, made of stone, which are now collectors' items.

A Keiller jar of the kind found by archaeologists on the site of the former Crosse & Blackwell factory in Charing Cross Road while the Tottenham Court Road Crossrail station was being built. Now a collector's item, this one is in a museum in New Zealand. (Collection of Auckland Museum Tamaki Paenga Hira, 1967.217, col.1940.1)

A Crosse & Blackwell label showing the factory's address, 21 Soho Square, above the site of the new Crossrail station.

10

CROSSRAIL ARCHAEOLOGY

'When the Metropolitan railway was cut in 1890 [anthrax] did emerge and it did kill people.'

LONDON'S LONG HISTORY

In about AD 50 the Roman occupiers built the first bridge across the Thames close to the present site of London Bridge, and from that moment London has been an important political, commercial and industrial centre. Moreover, from at least the time of Shakespeare it has been an important place of entertainment. One does not have to walk far in London to see evidence of its past: the remnants of the Roman wall, especially prominent near the Tower of London and at the Barbican; the Tower of London itself with its gruesome history; Marble Arch with its brass plaque reminding us of its former role as the site of Tyburn executions; the black circle markings on the courtyard outside the Guildhall to mark the site of the Roman arena; the Temple of Mithras, found in Walbrook in the 1950s and now within the Bloomberg Headquarters in Queen Victoria Street; nearby, in Cannon Street, the London Stone, supposedly left by Brutus, the entirely

London's Roman wall, built around AD 120. This remaining fragment is in the vicinity of the Tower of London. (Adam Bishop via Wikimedia Commons CC SA 3.0)

The site of Tyburn, scene of executions until 1783, when they were moved to Newgate, is marked by this plaque at Marble Arch. (Quodvultdeus via Wikimedia Commons CC SA 3.0)

The London Stone, set behind a grill at 111 Cannon Street, supposedly set by the Trojan Prince Brutus when he founded the city. (Lonpicman via Wikimedia Commons CC SA 3.0)

The Roman site of the Temple of Mithras, discovered in the city in the 1950s, is now within the Headquarters of Bloomberg in Queen Victoria Street. (Oxyman via Wikimedia Commons CC SA 2.0)

legendary Trojan founder of the city; the great arched roof of St Pancras station from which Eurostar trains now leave for the continent; and others far too numerous to mention.

HAPPY ARCHAEOLOGISTS

So when the Crossrail engineers proposed to remove 3 million tons of earth from beneath London and rather more than that in building new stations and other essential works on the surface, a smile crossed the faces of London's archaeologists, based at the Museum of London. Over 200 archaeologists have worked on the construction sites since the project was first conceived, and they were not to be disappointed as the engineers bored through the distinctive layers of London's past. Some of the discoveries were interesting and many were gruesome, with more than 10,000 objects being identified and retrieved. With the exception of some ancient amber and animal bones, the objects are housed in the Museum of London's Archaeological Archive in Hackney where they are available for research. The archaeologists' work began in 2004, four years before the passing of the Crossrail Bill, as bore holes were sunk to ascertain the geology of the route. This helped to identify the sites that were likely to be of greatest interest to the archaeologists. Much of the tunnelling is at depths of 30–40m, whereas most evidence of human occupation of London from prehistoric, Roman, mediaeval and later times is found in the first 9m. For this reason it was in the excavations for the stations, dug from the surface, and in the grouting shafts which were bored to stabilise ground (see compensation grouting in chapter 9), rather than in the tunnels, that most items of archaeological value were found. As each station was built the archaeologists were accommodated by the engineers and given months to complete their work before engineering works reinterred the sites.

STONE AGE AND BRONZE AGE LONDON

At Plumstead, where *Sophia* and *Mary* began their journey to North Woolwich in 2013, archaeologists found wooden stakes which had been shaped using a metal axe, probably made of bronze and dating back to about 2,000 BC. They may have marked the course of a bronze age pathway. At North Woolwich on the northern bank of the Thames, where *Sophia* and *Mary* emerged in 2014, there was evidence of a much older Mesolithic (Middle Stone Age) community close to the river, with traces of fires and collections of flint which was being used to make flint tools. These could be dated to about 6,000 BC. Even older remains were found when the new Canary Wharf station was being excavated. A piece of amber (fossilised tree resin) was

A woolly mammoth, much like the one whose jawbone was discovered during excavations on the Crossrail route and is now at the Natural History Museum. This specimen is in a museum in Germany. (Lou.gruber via Wikimedia Commons)

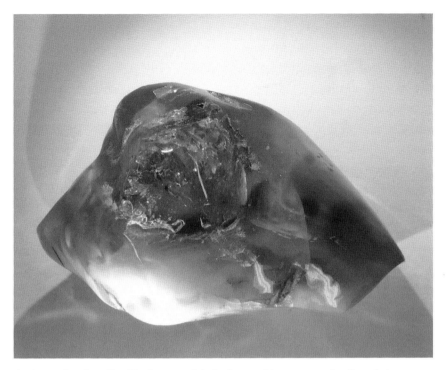

A piece of amber (fossilised tree resin) similar to this one was also found close to the site of the Canary Wharf Crossrail station; it too is now in the Natural History Museum. (Hannes Grobe via Wikimedia Commons CC SA 2.5)

found whose age was estimated as 55 million years. A jaw bone from a woolly mammoth was also unearthed, the mammoth dating from the last Ice age, which prevailed between 12,000 and 100,000 years ago. Dating from the same era, a prehistoric site was identified near the Royal Oak portal, close to the original channel of the Westbourne River, much of which now flows through pipes to the Thames, surfacing in Hyde Park as the Serpentine and passing over the trains at Sloane Square Underground station in a metal tube. The Royal Oak site revealed bones of large mammals including bison and reindeer that had been gnawed by carnivores. The amber and animal bones have been given to the Natural History Museum in Kensington.

BEDLAM AND THE PLAGUE

One of the most productive sites was in the vicinity of Liverpool Street station in the heart of the City. The subterranean area is roughly delineated by the present sites of Finsbury Circus, the Broadgate retail and office complex, and Liverpool Street station. More than 3,000 skeletons were unearthed close to the present site of the station. They had been interred at the New Churchyard burial ground, which was used between 1569 and 1739, as churchyard burial grounds in the City became full. It was also used by the St Mary Bethlehem Hospital, better known as Bedlam. This had been founded in 1247 as a priory and a centre for collecting alms for the poor, who were also housed there. In the following century it became a hospital for 'distracted' (mentally ill) patients, and in the reign of Henry VIII its administration was passed to the City of London at the request of the Lord Mayor, Sir John Gresham. From this time until the mid-eighteenth century the New Churchyard burial ground was used as a cemetery both for Bedlam and for the burial of bodies that could not be accommodated in the City's overcrowded churchyards as the population of London grew. By this time Bedlam was principally associated with the care of the insane and was visited by Londoners curious to observe the behaviour of the residents in what one historian of London has called a 'freakshow'. The hospital was rebuilt in St George's Fields, south London in the nineteenth century and survives as Bethlem Royal Hospital in West Wickham, in the London Borough of Bromley. It was the first hospital in Europe to specialise in mental illness.

Anaylsis of the bones recovered from the Crossrail excavations by archaeologists revealed that many of the skeletons were those of relatively young people who had moved to the capital as it expanded but had no resistance to the diseases associated with the crowded and insanitary conditions encountered in the city. Syphilis, tuberculosis and plague were particularly prevalent amongst the young migrants. It had long been supposed that the New Churchyard had been used for the burial of plague victims during the epidemic of 1665 and analysis of bones of that period did indeed reveal the presence in them of the

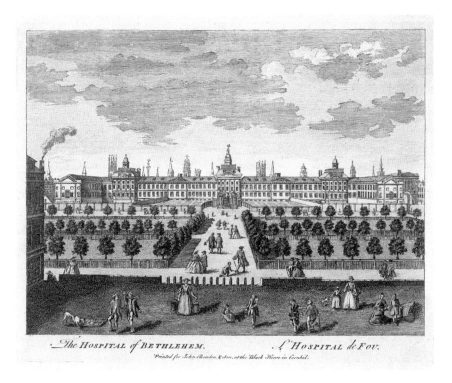

The HOSPITAL _of_ BETHLEHEM.　　　　_L'_ HOSPITAL _de_ FOU.

Printed for John Bowles & Son, at the Black Horse in Cornhill.

The Hospital of Bethlehem, or Bedlam, at Moorfields, was a hospital for the poor, then later for the mentally ill, and eventually became a 'freakshow', in the words of one historian, before its removal to south London. It was the site of many skeletons of victims of syphilis, tuberculosis and plague, discovered by archaeologists during excavations of Crossrail sites at Liverpool Street station. (Wellcome Images)

agent that causes bubonic plague: *Yersinia Pestis*. Many of the plague victims were buried in coffins and carefully laid to rest east to west in accordance with Christian custom, which contradicts the evidence of writers like Daniel Defoe, who claimed that 'they died by heaps and were buried by heaps'. But Defoe was only 5 years old and must have based his *Journal of the Plague Year* on the accounts of others. Studies of the teeth showed evidence of poor dental hygiene, some of it arising from poor diet including sugar which, though rich in energy from carbohydrates, was also the cause of dental decay, as it still is.

The area was marshy during the Middle Ages and froze in winter. The London historian William Fitzstephen described how, in the twelfth century, young men would tie animal bones to their feet and use them to skate on the frozen marsh so it was not surprising when such skates, formed from animal bones, were found in the area by the Crossrail archaeologists. They also discovered pilgrim badges indicating that their owners had made pilgrimages to destinations such as the shrine at Walsingham in Norfolk and Tours in France.

About 25,000 people were eventually buried in the New Churchyard and from 1635 it was managed by a family called Clitherow who profited from payments for the digging of graves and the installation of vaults. The Clitherows also had a sideline in carving and selling bone artefacts, many of the offcuts being found on the site during the Crossrail excavations. During the nineteenth century the area of the New Churchyard was used for the sites of Broad Street (closed in 1986 and later demolished) and Liverpool Street stations.

THE CROSSRAIL SKULLS

A more mysterious, and possibly more ominous discovery was also made in the vicinity of Liverpool Street station – more than fifty human skulls with few signs of bodies attached to them. They were not the first such discovery. In 1928 nine had been found during building work at the Bank of England and altogether about 300 skulls have been recovered from the vicinity of the Walbrook river. The Liverpool Street find had a strange gender imbalance, with twenty-five identified as male and five as female skulls. One possibility was that they had once been attached to skeletons but that during heavy rains and floods in the flat terrain which is characteristic of the area, they had simply been washed away from graveyards as skulls, being light and bulky, are more easily moved in water than the long, slender bones of arms and legs. The construction of the Roman wall in the area in about AD 200 appears to have been accompanied by the diversion (possibly accidentally) of the Walbrook. This short river, which is formed by the merger of two smaller steams near Finsbury

Circus, flowed through Roman London and enters the Thames near Southwark bridge. Its name probably arises from the fact that it flowed beneath the Roman wall whose construction caused it to flood and led to the creation of a marshy area, Moorfields, which lasted well throughout the mediaeval period and was finally drained in 1527. The wet terrain helped to preserve skulls and artefacts which the Crossrail archaeologists later disinterred. More than 100 Roman coins were discovered, dating from the time of Claudius, who conquered Britain in AD 43, to the later stages of the Roman occupation in AD 348.

But there may have been a sinister explanation for the skulls. They were all from the Londinium layers of the city, created during the period of Roman occupation between AD 43 and the departure of the Romans in AD 410. At first it was thought that the skulls dated

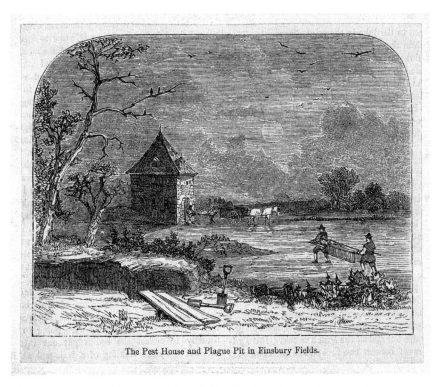

The Pest House and Plague Pit in Finsbury Fields.

The Pest House or Plague Pit, Moorfields, site also of a marshy area where young men would skate on frozen ground. Their bone skates were discovered during Crossrail work. (Wellcome Images)

from the destruction of Londinium by Boudicca (Boadicea) the Queen of the Iceni. According to the Roman historian Tacitus, in revenge for her humiliation by the Roman procurator (tax gatherer) Catus Decianus and the rape of her daughters, Boudicca attacked and destroyed Camulodunum (Colchester), Verulanium (St Albans) and finally London. These events occurred in 60 or 61 AD. The rebellion was finally ended by the Roman Governor Suetonius Paulinus at a battle probably fought at a place called Cuttle Mill on Watling Street (now the A5) between Towcester and Milton Keynes, but came close to toppling Roman rule in Britain.

According to legend, Boudicca is buried beneath platform 10 of King's Cross station, close to the *Harry Potter* exhibit at that London terminus. Boudicca was a favourite of the Victorians who saw her defiance of the mighty Roman Empire as foreshadowing the much

Boudicca, Queen of the Iceni, and her violated daughters. Her rebellion came close to ending Roman rule in Britain, and she was a heroine to the Victorians who subscribed for this statue on Westminster Bridge. (Lily15 via Wikimedia Commons CC SA 3.0)

greater British Empire over which Victoria reigned. The statue of Boudicca and her daughters was erected on Westminster Bridge in 1902 as a tribute to Victoria, shortly after her death the previous year. The discovery that the skulls were Roman victims of Boudicca's vengeance would have been, perhaps, a suitable salute to the East Anglian Queen by the heroic engineers of Crossrail.

Carbon dating, disappointingly, placed the skulls probably within the period AD 80–380, a little too late for Boudicca though firmly within the period of Roman settlement. Further efforts were made to date the skulls more accurately by the use of dendrochronology (tree ring dating) on timbers found with the skulls and these gave a date later than AD 120, about the time of the emperor Hadrian. This was a troublesome time for the Romans in Britain which prompted the construction of Hadrian's Wall on the Northern frontier. Perhaps this was an indication of more widespread turmoil reaching Londinium, since other investigations suggested that in AD 125 London was consumed by a severe fire, possibly instigated by rebellious Celts following the earlier example of Boudicca. Since many of the skulls were found along a roadway, apparently placed there with some care, they may have been trophies. Celts were known to display skulls in this ritualistic way but they may have been placed there by the Romans who put down the rebellion as a stern warning to others. The Roman wall around the city and delineating its square mile was possibly built as a consequence of these later insurrections.

EVERY CORNER OF THE EMPIRE

One of the most intriguing features of the skulls was that their owners were found to come from every corner of the empire with evidence of natives of Belgium, Spain, North Africa, Turkey, Greece and Rome itself. And they had not died natural deaths as they bore multiple wounds from a variety of swords, axes and other instruments sharp and blunt. The wide variety of their origins and the multiple wounds

suggested that they could have been gladiators whose grisly con-
tests would have been at the height of their popularity at the time of
Hadrian. If they are the skulls of gladiators, the arena whose bounda-
ries are marked out in the courtyard of Guildhall may mark the scene
of their violent deaths. But it was the habit of Romans to send to
its more remote territories legionaries from all over the empire,
thereby reducing the likelihood of their becoming sympathetic to the
local population or forming coherent groups amongst themselves in
opposition to the remote authority of Rome. So perhaps they were
legionaries killed by the Celts in the uprising which produced the fire.
We will probably never know for certain.

MORE PLAGUE VICTIMS

On 15 March 2013 – ominously, the Ides of March in the thirteenth
year of the millennium – it was announced that Crossrail excavations had unearthed twenty-three skeletons in a burial ground in
Farringdon. They were discovered during the sinking of a grouting
shaft (see chapter 9) to stabilise surrounding buildings.

The discovery was not a surprise. In 1348 Sir Walter de Manny, a
knight of Edward III, purchased 13 acres of ground to bury victims
of the plague which, in the particularly virulent outbreak of that
year, killed more than a third of the population. In the sixteenth
century John Stow, historian of London, had claimed that 150,000
victims of the Black Death (later identified as bubonic plague) had
been buried in London, many of them on a site known as No Man's
Land in Farringdon. The Crossrail skeletons were on the edge of
Charterhouse Square, Smithfield, just to the south of Farringdon.
Moreover, the location of the graves, the early fourteenth century
pottery found with the skeletons and the way the graves were laid
out (similarly to those on a plague cemetery discovered nearby in
the 1980s) suggested that this was indeed a plague burial ground and
very probably the No Man's Land site purchased by de Manny and
referred to by Stow.

Analysis of the bones, dating from the fourteenth century, yielded traces of the plague pathogen *Yersinia Pestis*, which had been responsible for the epidemic. The skeletons also showed evidence of rickets, a condition caused by poor nutrition and in particular by a shortage of vitamin D. One of the consequences of the fourteenth-century plague was a shortage of labour, encouraging country dwellers to seek higher wages and a better life elsewhere, so it is interesting that further analysis of ten skeletons suggested that four were of individuals born in eastern, central or northern England, indicating that even in the Middle Ages London attracted migrants in search of a more prosperous life.

In 1370 a Carthusian monastery (the Charterhouse) was founded by de Manny in the area and it remained there until brutally suppressed by Henry VIII, after which it eventually became the home, for over two centuries, of Charterhouse School which moved to Godalming, Surrey, in 1872. The remaining buildings, restored after

Charterhouse Square, near Farringdon Crossrail station, site of a monastery, burial ground, school and home for elderly citizens. Many of the skeletons found on the site were those of migrants to London in the Middle Ages. (Paul the Archivist via Wikimedia Commons CC SA 4.0)

wartime destruction, house Charterhouse Pensioners, known as Brothers, forty in number and some of them now women. To qualify they must be at least 60 years old, single and of limited means, have lived in the UK for at least two years and value companionship.

A GREATER THREAT

Bubonic plague has a very short life after the death of the victim and survives a matter of days following burial so there was no danger to the Crossrail tunnellers or to the residents of Farringdon from the newly discovered plague graves. Anthrax, however, is a different matter and the Farringdon area is again the potential victim. In June 2009 the BBC reported that evidence was presented to the Select Committee on the Crossrail Bill that there was a large burial site close to the planned Crossrail site at Farringdon. It was suggested that it contained victims of both bubonic plague and anthrax, the latter having been taken to Smithfield in 1520 in some contaminated meat,

The drinking fountain at Smithfield, once a cattle market, then a meat market and one-time burial ground for victims of bubonic plague and anthrax – but happily no longer a threat to Crossrail's engineers or archaeologists. (Justinc via Wikimedia Commons CC SA 2.0)

wiping out the local population. It was further claimed that when the Metropolitan Railway was cut in 1890, Anthrax did claim victims. This, though alarming, is more doubtful since the dates are wrong: the Metropolitan Railway was built in the 1860s not 1890, and the City & South London Railway, which did open in 1890, is nowhere near Smithfield. The committee was assured by the QC who was acting on behalf of the Department of Transport, which was promoting the Crossrail Bill, that there was 'literally an aircraft hangar full of reports on Crossrail', and that 'scary headlines' were not wanted! In due course the human and animal remains found during exploratory tunnelling for Crossrail were examined and traces of neither bubonic plague nor anthrax were found. Relief all round!

STEPNEY MANOR HOUSE

The stretch between Pudding Mill Lane, near the Olympic Park, and Stepney Green yielded some interesting remnants of mediaeval London. Pudding Mill Lane is close to the River Lea, whose adjacent meadows furnished grazing for animals while the river itself powered flour mills and provided fish for the local community. Wooden structures were recovered which are thought to be the remains of weirs to catch the fish.

The more striking discovery, however, revealed a substantial moated manor house dating from the fifteenth century. It lay to the west of the historic church of St Dunstan, sometimes called the Sailors' Church because it was the first church seen by sailors passing along the Thames to the City of London. The manor house belonged to the Fenne family and furnished evidence of their wealthy lifestyle in the form of elegant Venetian glass and ornaments for clothing and footwear. From the early 1600s it was the property of the Marquis of Worcester and became known as Worcester House. He supported the King during the Civil War and the house was later confiscated and given to Maurice Thompson, a supporter of Parliament and a leading puritan. He established a college, church and school, parts of which survived until they were bombed in the Second World War.

Four tons of bricks were reclaimed from the manor by the Crossrail work and given to English Heritage for use in the restoration of the brickwork of Tudor buildings. Part of the site is now occupied by Stepney City Farm.

SHIPS, BRIDGES AND FOOTBALL

A short distance north-east of the Connaught tunnel, the line enters the Crossrail tunnel in the Limmo Peninsula in which *Elizabeth* and *Victoria* began their journey towards Farringdon in November and December 2012. This was the former site of the Thames Ironworks which has a place both in industrial history and the history of football. The Thames Ironworks & Shipbuilding Company, to give it its full title, was founded in 1837 and was one of the first to use iron rather than wood for the building of ships. It produced 144 warships in its seventy-five years including one of the first iron-clads for the Royal Navy, *HMS Warrior* which, when launched in 1860, was the fastest warship afloat. She was preserved and is now to be found in Portsmouth along with Nelson's *Victory* and Henry VIII's ill-fated *Mary Rose*. The company also made a private yacht for Queen Victoria and components for Brunel's Albert Bridge across the Tamar, Blackfriars Railway Bridge and Hammersmith Suspension Bridge. One of its most unusual commissions, successfully completed in 1877, was to build the special vessel that brought the obelisk Cleopatra's Needle from Egypt to London for its installation on the Victoria Embankment. It only just made it, being nearly lost in a storm in the Bay of Biscay.

In 1895 Thames Ironworks Football Club was established on the initiative of the company's managing director, Arnold Hills, for the company's workers, the club's crest consisting of crossed riveters' hammers, marked with the letters TIW. They competed successfully for five years and in 1900 the club decided that, to progress further, they would need to engage professional players. The club was therefore dissolved in June and, a month later, became West Ham United football club. It is from the crest of crossed hammers that is

HMS *Warrior*, one of the
first ironclads in the Royal
Navy, built at Thames
Ironworks and, at the time
of her launch, the fastest
ship afloat. She now sits
in Portsmouth Dockyard
with Nelson's *Victory* and
Henry VIII's *Mary Rose*.
(Geni via Wikimedia
Commons CC SA 4.0)

Cleopatra's Needle
rises from the Victoria
Embankment, after being
brought from Egypt in a
vessel specially constructed
for the purpose by Thames
Ironworks. (Adrian
Pingstone via Wikimedia
Commons)

derived the name *The Hammers* and not, as it often believed, from West Ham where they were based. The club moved to The Boleyn Ground in 1904 where many spectators continued to refer to them as 'The Irons' and remained there until their move to the Olympic stadium in 2016. The club joined the football league in 1919 and has produced many international players including three of England's 1966 World Cup Winners.

Closure

The works produced 144 warships altogether, including two for the Japanese Navy that defeated the Russians in the war of 1904–05. In 1912, as orders for ships were proving hard to come by, Hills petitioned the First Lord of the Admiralty, Winston Churchill, for more orders for the Royal Navy. He was unsuccessful and the yard closed the same year. If the yard had survived for two more years it would have benefited from orders for war materials for the First World War. Crossrail archaelogists found remains of the shipyards and the ironworks including a halfpenny coin dated 1862 which was found close to one of the slipways from which ships were launched. Many of the bricks found on the site were firebricks from Scotland and from Blaydon, on the Tyne, while others, of unknown origin, bear the same maker's marks as those used at Alcatraz Prison in San Francisco Harbor, their origins a mystery.

WESTBOURNE PARK: BRUNEL'S GWR DEPOT

The Great Western Railway's first London terminus, at Paddington, entered service in 1838 but was replaced in 1854 by Isambard Kingdon Brunel's more imposing structure which we still have today. A depot and workshops were built nearby, at Westbourne Park, where engines were housed and serviced. The Crossrail excavations revealed a huge engine shed, workshops and turntables for the steam engines. By the end of the nineteenth century, as rail traffic approached its peak, a further depot was built at Old Oak Common, a little further along

A locomotive turntable in use at Swanage. The ones at Old Oak Common were much larger and used, as here, to turn steam locomotives for a return journey in the days before multiple units, in which the driver simply moves from one end of the train to the other, as with the 345 Crossrail trains. (Peter Langsdale via Wikimedia Commons CC SA 2.0)

the main line. It was the largest in the world and could accommodate over 100 locomotives. Some parts of it remained in use until 2009 when it was closed to make way for the new Crossrail depot which will occupy the site.

11

CROSSRAIL: THE FUTURE

A LONG GESTATION

And so Crossrail is born at last after a gestation that, as we have seen, can be traced back to the Second World War. Henceforward we have to remember to call it the Elizabeth Line. In 1863 the world's first underground railway, the Metropolitan, entered service during the reign of Queen Elizabeth II's long-reigning great-great-grandmother whose name was adopted by the Victoria Line in 1968. And now an even longer-reigning queen has given her name to the main-line underground railway in her capital. And the new railway, as it gradually enters service, will be judged by its achievements rather than its promise; by the number of passengers it conveys safely and comfortably to their destinations. Under present plans, more traffic is likely to pass eastwards than will pass westwards, making less than optimum use of expensive tunnels. A remedy would be to create an additional link to the west via Willesden to Northampton and Milton Keynes. This would also help to relieve the congested suburban services out of Euston in preparation for the projected HS2 services from that station.

SOUTHAMPTON TO CAMBRIDGE

But that is not the end of the story of main-line trains crossing London. The north–south Thameslink service from St Pancras via Blackfriars to destinations in south London, Surrey, Kent and Sussex will undergo a major upgrade in 2019 with twenty-four trains an hour between St Pancras and Blackfriars at peak periods, a new entrance to Blackfriars station on the south bank of the Thames and a transformation of London Bridge station which has taken eight often troubled years. It is already being suggested that direct Crossrail services could be extended to Ebbsfleet, an entity which suddenly appeared in the vicinity of Dartford as a railway station on the Eurostar service from London to the Continent and has its own football team but which is hard to find on a road map. And plans are already being made for Crossrail 2, which has been under discussion since a Chelsea–Hackney Line was mooted in the 1970s to connect those two populous districts of London which are ill-served by train services. Proposals have gone though many stages of consultation since that time, as Crossrail 1 did, but the latest proposals are for an underground link which would connect Surrey to Hertfordshire. It would enter a portal north of Wimbledon and pass via Balham, Clapham Junction and a new station called King's Road Chelsea on to Victoria and Tottenham Court Road and thence to a station serving Euston and St Pancras for a connection to the HS2 service. From there it would proceed to Angel and Dalston after which it would become two branches: one would pass via Seven Sisters before emerging from a portal at New Southgate and the other from a portal at Tottenham Hale. The tunnels would be 37km in length, compared to the 42km for Crossrail 1. At the southern end there would be links to the very busy South Western Railway network, stretching as far as Southampton, and in the north to the West Anglia network and on to Cambridge with its rapidly expanding economy and overstretched transport system. The estimated cost at 2014 prices is £32.1 billion, twice that of Crossrail 1, but it is estimated that the service, with up to thirty trains an hour, would add

10 per cent to London's rail capacity and pay for itself by generating taxes from the 200,000 new jobs it would help to create, many of them outside the capital.

This is the plan that is reflected in the draft transport strategy of the Mayor of London, Sadiq Khan, published in June 2017. By 2041 he wants 80 per cent of trips in the capital to be made by foot, bicycle or public transport in order to 'help address many of London's health problems by reducing activity and cleaning up the air'. And he suggests that this 'can only be achieved through building new lines and in particular Crossrail 2'. When the Transport Secretary, Chris Grayling, expressed his support for Crossrail 2 it attracted criticism from the Mayor of Greater Manchester, Andy Burnham, who drew attention to the government's decision to cancel rail electrification plans in the Regions and raised questions about the government's declared intention to rebalance the economy away from the capital. Steve Rotherham, his opposite number in Liverpool, made similar criticisms. Further delays in the plan may be confidently anticipated!

We can only wish the mayors and their successors well in what will no doubt be a long, arduous and argumentative process.

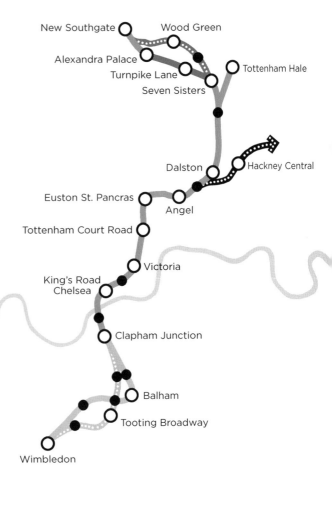

○ Stations

● Intermediate Shaft

▬▬ Central core of route

▫▫▫ Route previously consulted on via Tooting Broadway

▬▬ Newly proposed route

▪▪▪ Potential future Eastern branch

▬▬ Option via Turnpike Lane and Alexandra Palace

▫▫▫ Option via Wood Green

New Southgate

Wood Green

Alexandra Palace

Turnpike Lane

Seven Sisters

Tottenham Hale

Dalston

Hackney Central

Euston St. Pancras

Angel

Tottenham Court Road

Victoria

King's Road Chelsea

Clapham Junction

Balham

Tooting Broadway

Wimbledon

POSTSCRIPT

In September 2018 Crossrail announced that the date for the commencement of Crossrail services would be postponed from December 2018 to the autumn of 2019, with no date specified. So Her Majesty the Queen now has a diary vacancy for 9 December 2018. It also seems that the cost may increase from £14.8 billion to £15.4 billion. However, since the original estimate was almost £16 billion and was revised down by the government spending review in 2010 by accounting sorcery, this is not too bad, particularly given the heroic nature of the project. And although the delay to opening is disappointing, it was not entirely unexpected. It has been suggested for some time that there have been problems completing some of the stations in the central area and that many difficulties have occurred in making the state-of-the-art signalling and safety systems used in the trains compatible with existing signalling and communication equipment using older technology on the tracks. As long ago as January 2015 the project chairman was talking of a 'mitigation plan' to deal with signalling problems (see chapter 8, pp 134–5) but presumably this plan was not adequate for the task. Crossrail will no doubt occupy many more column inches in newspapers before it finally becomes the Elizabeth Line. Watch this space.

Printed in Great Britain
by Amazon

17865774R00105